BORN FOR BATTLE

ABOUT THE AUTHOR

A child of CIM missionaries,
Arthur Mathews spent his childhood
in China and grew to manhood
as a farmhand in Australia.
While Melbourne Bible Institute
gave him his formal training, the Lord
trained him through a continuing
study of His Word and through
a lifetime of experiences and testings:
during his years, for instance,
as a missionary in China's interior,
his service in the Indian Army
during World War II, four years of
house arrest with his wife and baby
in Communist China (the story is
told in *Green Leaf in Drought Time*
by Isobel Kuhn), his many years
as a leader in the Overseas Missionary
Fellowship, and through his last
battle, the suffering and wasting of
amyotrophic lateral sclerosis.
He died in July 1978 at 66.

Born for Battle
R. Arthur Mathews

OMF BOOKS
U.S.A.: 404 South Church Street, Robesonia, PA 19551
U.K.: Belmont, The Vine, Sevenoaks, Kent TN13 3TZ

STL BOOKS
P.O. Box 48 Bromley, Kent, U.K.

CONTENTS

Foreword

During the time of my pastorate at Moody Memorial Church, Chicago, Arthur and Wilda Mathews came to the city to take on the work of OMF representative in the Midwest. Arthur Mathews' presence in the area at such a time was a great encouragement to me, and although the family did not attend Moody Church, we had many opportunities for fellowship and friendship. Because of this my love for the man grew and my appreciation of his spiritual depth and strength increased, for I knew the experiences through which he had passed in China and saw the impact they had made on his life.

It was this imprint of the Master's hand, made through suffering and testing, that reflected Christ, not only in Arthur's life, but also in the editorials he wrote for *East Asia Millions*. Having read these edition by edition for many years, I came to realize increasingly what a man of vision, depth, perception, and godly insight he was.

How thankful I am, therefore, that before the Lord called Arthur to His immediate presence, he collected so many of these articles, plus additional material, and has shared them with what one trusts will be a much wider public. The whole tone of these chapters is one which is sadly missing today, when Christian living is made such a

happy-go-lucky experience, with the empty promise of "all problems solved once you are saved." As
the age of grace draws to its conclusion and the
coming of the Lord is an ever-approaching hope,
so Satan crowds on all pressure—and how few of
God's people know how to resist him in the Name
of the Lord!

Arthur Mathews was indeed a man born for
battle. With penetrating insight he says in this
book, "The thing that we need to be afraid of
today is that the spirit that produces world trends
should invade Christ's mighty army and argue us
off the offensive into a compromised coexistence
with the world's attitudes—so that we end up just
like the world, taking lessons in French and practicing detente." It can truly be said of Arthur, "I
fought long and hard for my Lord, and through it
all I have kept true to Him; and now the time has
come for me to stop fighting and rest" (2 Tim.
4:7—LB).

My prayer is that this book may not only have a
wide circulation, but that it may become
prescribed reading for all young believers, especially those contemplating ministry, either in the
homelands or overseas.

                              ALAN REDPATH, D.D., F.C.A.
Willow Beck Cottage
Capernwray Hall
Carnforth, England

Preface

It was not the presumptuous heart of the author that conceived the idea of adding another volume to the libraries of Christian books. The pressure was put on me from many who through the years have been reading my editorials in *East Asia Millions* (the magazine put out by the Overseas Missionary Fellowship). These friends have been insistent that the editorials should be put into a more permanent form. Others, too, have been praying the project might become reality.

But beside the urging of friends, there is also a compelling motive in my own heart that will not be gainsaid. This constraint puts an urgency on me that is best described in the words of God's Old Testament prophets, "the burden of the Lord." My burden relates to the flood of evil that the devil is pouring into the world and, at the same time, the passivity of many of God's saints as they view this state of affairs and their ignorance of the part God expects them to play in His warfare against Satan. Because the devil knows his time is running out, he is concentrating all he has got in a desperate last-ditch attempt to defeat the purposes of God. Surely this is not the time for God's soldiers to withdraw into passivity, to put reality out of their minds. To my way of thinking, it takes conflict and the fact of an enemy to put prayer in perspective as a significant factor in furthering the cause of Christ in the world. On the other side of the coin, it takes an understanding of objective truth, as God has given it to us in the Bible, for the believer to stand in victory and resist the devil.

Not for nothing did I list the 12th Frontier Force Regiment as my first choice when I was commissioned in the Indian Army during World War II. I am sure that God was in that choice. The regimental center was in the town of Sialkot, in what is now Pakistan, but what was then known as the Punjab. It was in Sialkot that revival broke out at the turn of the century, through the prayers of Praying Hyde and the leaders of the Punjab Prayer Union. I am not trying to claim prayer-power by association with this great prayer warrior. But I can assure you that no one who reads his biography will be the same afterwards as to his practice of and outlook on prayer.

Over the years I have dug deeply into my books on prayer and copied helpful thoughts into my Bible and used them widely in messages. As it never occurred to me that one day I would be writing a book, I have not kept a record of all the sources from which I have borrowed bricks to build up my own house of faith. Nebuchadnezzar stamped all his bricks with his name, but all my bricks, from whatever source they have come, carry the impress of the Holy Spirit, otherwise they would have been discarded long ago. So here I take up my pen to discharge "the burden of the Lord" in the *'paracletism'* of the Holy Spirit.

R. ARTHUR MATHEWS

1

The Soldier of the Cross

It was a sad day for Adam, and for the rest of us, when his comfortable life in the Garden of Eden came to a sudden end. Though Adam was created to have dominion, his choice to disobey God changed everything. His status as royalty over God's creation was lost, and he became a bond-slave of sin and a wage-earner on Satan's terms. By his act of disobedience Adam yielded his kingship to Satan, who from then on claimed the dominion offered by man's disobedience and became "the prince of this world." In Eden God decreed enmity between the serpent's seed and the seed of the woman. Because of this, the law of strife became the law of life for the human race. Hereafter the sinister eye of the deceiver would be on perpetual alert for evidences of the arrival of the Seed in order to lay plans to prevent the coming of this one who was to crush his head.

In the fullness of God's time the Lord Jesus Christ, the Seed of the woman and the eternal Son of God, was born. As the Son of Man on earth, Jesus was no mere civilian passively suffering the attacks and harassment of Satan. He was the

Pioneer and Captain of our salvation, the original Soldier of the Cross, pressing forward along the lonely road to victory through the sufferings of death. Nailing His feet to that Cross could not prevent Him from crushing Satan's head beneath His heel. And with His nail-pierced hands He tore off from Himself the evil powers that attempted to prevent Him from ascending to the throne.

Now glorified and seated at the Father's right hand, "far above all principality, and power, and might, and dominion," Jesus as Lord of all is beyond reach of Satan's attacks. The finished work of Calvary is now completely unassailable. Nothing that Satan may do can change the finality of the victory stroke that crushed his head.

However, the implication of that victory over the powers of evil and its application in the world of men is now in the hands of the Church on earth. Consequently, the bitter enmity of Satan is now directed against the Church in order to vent his spleen against the Head through the members of His Body. In his true character as adversary Satan is very much alive to rob the finished work of Christ of its full effect among men. His fiery darts zero in on the members of Christ's Body who have not learned to take their position in the heavenly places with Christ by faith and who face life without taking to themselves by prayer the whole armor of God. He is especially concerned about those who are proclaiming the Good News of the finished work of Christ in earth's dark corners.

Because of the hostility of the devil, the work of conforming the members of Christ's Body to the likeness of the soldier-image of the Head is high on the priority list of the Holy Spirit. As believers we are in Christ and He in us, and this means that His aggression against Satan must be expressed through us. So we are no longer free to play the role of civilians, living as if there were no war.

Our soldier role is pictured for us throughout the Old Testament and is now established by our union with our conquering Head and affirmed in the New Testament. The history of the saints in every age is one of conflict. The pathway the disciple treads as he follows His Lord is one of certain warfare.

At this point let us ask ourselves some serious questions:

- Am I expressing the enmity God put between the devil and the Church's Head?
- Or, am I seeking detente, coexistence, and peace through compromise?
- Am I available to my Lord as a willing instrument, ready for His use in His warfare?
- Am I aware of the teaching of Scripture about my part in the spiritual conflict?

It has been said that "the battle of Waterloo was won on the playing fields of Eton." The essential principles that brought about the defeat of Napoleon were developed on the football field. Had there been no football-field discipline, there could have been very different results at Waterloo. The schoolboy playing for his school learns that the will of the individual must be subservient at all times to the will of his captain. He plays to give all that he has for the glory of his side, not just to win a name for himself.

It might appear to border on impudence to transfer the thought and say that the battle of the Cross was won on the *praying* field of Gethsemane, but I am serious. If not actually in terms of encounter with the enemy, then from the point of vital principle, it was most certainly so.

The Soldier of the Cross had taught His disciples the need to pray, "Thy will be done on earth as it is in heaven." The obvious inference is that God has limited certain of His activities to responding to the prayers of His people. Unless they pray, He will not act. Heaven may will something to happen, but heaven waits and encourages earth's initiative to desire that will, and then to will and pray that it happens. The will of God is not done on earth by an inexorable, juggernaut omnipotence "out there" overriding or ignoring the will of man on earth. On the contrary, God has willed that His hand be held back while He seeks for a man, an intercessor to plead, "Thy will be done on earth," in this or that specific situation.

The Cross of Jesus Christ represents the one focal point in history at which the redemptive work of God for man focused and culminated in one infinite, massive act. Gethsemane represents the vital principle which makes it possible for that redemptive work to be successfully consummated on earth. So let us deepen our consideration of this "infinite, massive act."

On the road to the Cross the Savior is seen as passive, a man acted upon, not a man active. He was taken, led away, scourged, spat upon, and finally nailed to the Cross. He was "brought as a lamb to the slaughter/A victim led, His blood was shed." The Lamb of God was a victim caught in the squeeze between the good and acceptable and perfect will of God and the evil will of heartless men.

In the quiet solitude of Gethsemane's olive grove Jesus appears in an active role. If He is acted upon on Golgotha, He is the lead actor in Gethsemane. It is here that He sets Himself to endure the travail pains of a demanding prayer warfare and actively wills for God to do His work through Him, regardless of the cost to Himself. His troubled spirit expresses itself in groans, strong crying and tears. The battle is joined. The intensity mounts. Heaven's legions press forward to help, but this is not their battlefield; it is His alone. His will is assailed at every point. "His sweat was as it were great drops of blood falling down to the ground." Here is God's work being done in God's way. God willing it in heaven, and a man willing it on earth. The sacrifice at Calvary happened because first, out of His soul's depths in dark Gethsemane, the Soldier of the Cross wills with God for it to happen. As His prayer groans upward, "Thy will be done," the determinate counsel of the Father moves to the sacrifice of His Lamb. The Soldier of the Cross wins His battle in the praying field of Gethsemane with only a sentence prayer, but it involved His life. There the embattled Savior knelt and "fired the shot heard round the world"—"Thy will be done."

In His Gethsemane struggle the Lord Jesus teaches us two important things: "Submit to God" and "resist the devil." God's warfare against Satan is carried on by His submissive people actively resisting Satan by insisting at all costs, "Thy will be done on earth as it is in heaven."

> *Who wills with God will pray and find*
> *God fights His battles through self's will resigned.*

PRAYER:
   Oh Lord! help me to accept the fact that I am born for battle and am responsible to seek the doing of the will of my Father on earth by resisting the enemy's attempts to reverse that will. To this end I pray that the will to disentangle myself from the smothering absorption of civilian living may be strengthened in me, so that I may be a good soldier of Jesus Christ. And "Oh, may no coward spirit seek to leaven the Warrior code, the calling that is ours."

2

The Soldier's Best Friend

The first duty of a soldier is obedience. The most evident duty of a soldier is to endure hardness. The ultimate duty of a soldier is to offer the supreme sacrifice.

D. M. M'intyre

If we accept the fact that our role in life is that of soldiers, then we must drop our toys and become more acquainted with the weapons of our warfare. In a conflict situation a soldier's best friend is his weapon, because it is his one resource for disposing of the enemy, securing his own safety, and accomplishing the will of his captain.

In the account of the Lord Jesus' meeting Satan in the temptation in the wilderness, the Holy Spirit has given us a good example of how we as Christians are to conduct ourselves against the same evil power that is alive and active in the world today. But before considering the actual combat situation, we need to look first at the condition of Jesus and the factors in His life that made Him ready to face His enemy.

Luke is careful to tell us that Jesus was filled with the Spirit as He was led into the wilderness.

The choice to go off into the wilds and have a bash at the devil was not made by Jesus Himself. He was "led of the Spirit." And please do not think that this is not really relevant to what awaited Him. It is important that Jesus was obediently and willingly submissive to a higher control. His heart was completely devoid of the least suggestion of presumption. And this is different from many who seek fame and advertise themselves as having power over the devil. The arena for the conflict of Jesus is not advertised in the *Jerusalem Times* to attract the sensation-hungry crowds to the grand-stand of the surrounding wilderness hills. Submissive to the will of the Holy Spirit of God, Jesus is led away from the haunts of men. Confrontation with the devil is not to be sought presumptuously, nor is it to be entered into under conditions in which the individual is not filled with the Spirit.

The fact that He was led to a place where for forty days He had no food could easily have raised problems in the mind of Jesus. In the same situation we would have all sorts of arguments about the unreasonableness of being expected to endure such hardship. But God's soldier must be able to endure hardness and to learn how to keep under the clamorous hungers of the flesh if he is to be a good soldier. Bodily appetites are insistent for attention and give the devil a good vantage point if they are not kept under control. The crafty enemy has had centuries of experience in finding the best openings to get man to move out of God's will and choose his own. He knows how to play on our natural hunger pangs and take advantage of them to achieve his ends. We are almost forced to believe that Satan purposely waited until Jesus was at the limit of His physical endurance, thereby hoping that His powers of resistance would be weakened and unable to cope with a frontal attack.

There is something else that we must take notice of because of its relevance to the actual conflict with Satan. For Jesus, the silent years at Nazareth must have been filled with more than the toil of a carpenter. Part of His qualifications for service lay in the fact that He had filled a place in the secular world among the people of His own town and had earned from them the distinction of being "the carpenter." But Jesus did not stop at the mere fulfilling of the secular responsibilities as the carpenter, exhausting though that might have been; He stretched Himself at all times to fill His mind with the treasures of the Word of God.

These are the factors that are preliminary to the actual conflict with Satan. And as we look at them, certain things stand out emphasizing *the condition* of Jesus as He was confronted by the devil.

- He was filled and controlled by the Holy Spirit. The initiative for the confrontation with the devil was not His; He was brought to it by the Spirit of God. These factors are prerequisites for victory over Satan.

- His mind was a storehouse of the words of God. For the Holy Spirit to wield His mighty sword effectively through a human instrument, He must first have absolute control of the instrument, and the mind of the man must be well stored with the words of God.

- His human body was starved to exhaustion, but not by His own choice. For Jesus the warrior's post may have been at starvation-point, but the warrior's position has not been compromised at any point. His value-system has not been changed even though His physical system is being "stabbed by all the swords of sense." As a good soldier He endures hardness and brings His body into subjection. Victory does not depend on physical fitness. But this does not mean that a body brought to a state of weakness by some self-imposed stunt will help the chances of victory.

Having studied carefully the condition of Jesus, we can now look at His *competence* in resisting and defeating Satan. At the first approach of the enemy, Jesus took the sword of the Spirit to be His one sure weapon, His best friend in this emergency. This sword so carefully "wrought and edged by the Holy Spirit Himself" is the utterance of God and is specially designed to resist and confound Satan and all His hosts of evil. And it is His weapon, for is it not called "the sword of the Spirit"? Therefore it is for Him to bring to the mind of the one He has led to this particular confrontation that specific utterance which He has wrought into the blade. In this case the specific word was from Deuteronomy 8:3: "Man shall not live by bread alone, but by every word (Gr. *rhema*) that proceedeth out of the mouth of God." We are all more familiar with the Greek word *logos* than *rhema*. The latter refers to a more specific utterance than the more general word *logos*.

Three times the Lord Jesus met the assaults of Satan in this way. Amazingly, all that it took to defeat the devil was "every word that proceedeth out of the mouth of God." Apart from this word "our striving would be losing." Victories over the devil are not won by having a Bible and knowing some of it. Nor are they won by resolutions and good intent. It takes the sword of the Spirit, God's specific utterance, thrust at the enemy in the power of the controlling Holy Spirit with an unashamed "It is written" and "Thus saith the Lord."

There is nothing that Jesus used to defeat Satan that is not available to us. Therefore, victory is as attainable for us as it was for Him. He was filled with the Spirit, and we are expressly commanded to "be filled with the Spirit." However, let no one think that a single experience of being filled exhausts the claim of this command on our obedience. The tense of the verb is continuous and means "be being filled." The condition of being filled with the Holy Spirit is something to which we are required to give constant attention. And then we too may have our minds filled with the Word of God. We dare not be careless or lazy about storing God's Word in our minds.

Let us not ignore the relation between condition and competence. If we would have competence in withstanding the attacks of the enemy, then let us look to our condition. Am I being led of the Spirit? Is He in complete control of my being? Am I diligently storing my mind with the Word of God? Then "the only thing that matters," says Amy Carmichael, "is to throw all the energies of our being into the faithful use of this precious blade." Then, and only then, may we "Rest our cause upon His holy Word."

3

Our Wrestling

"There wrestled a man with him"
(Genesis 32:24).

Our wrestling with the enemy can never hope
for victory unless this Man has first wrestled with
us, has dealt with all that hinders His control, and
has reduced us to complete surrender.

It is quite certain that in the spiritual warfare
nothing is achieved by activities which do not
bring us into close touch with the enemy. . . . For
where the devil's authority is challenged, where a
work is begun that will weaken his hold on the
hearts of men and deliver them from the thrall-
dom in which they were born, there the clash can
never be long averted, and we find ourselves
close-locked in a hand-to-hand encounter with
the forces of evil.

From the Report of the China Inland Mission, 1930

Our business, like any other, is to be learned by
constant practice and experience; and our experience is to be had in war, not at reviews.

Sir John Moore

"For we wrestle not. . . ." Having read as far as
the first four words of the Apostle Paul's

comments on the nature of the Christian's conflict,
I am tempted to stop and say to myself, How true!
"In an age of fops and toys" and a prevailing
subjective and utilitarian climate of thought, wrestling, in the spiritual sense, is not listed among the
activities of many of our churches. We petition, we
sing our praises, and have our pot-luck dinners,
but the kind of wrestling that Paul is referring to
is not usually included.

However, having said that, I hasten to correct
myself. We do wrestle, but it is the wrestling of
Jacob. When God grapples with us in order to
break the spirit of self-sufficiency that rides high
in our hearts and to transform us into His Israels,
we struggle against His efforts.

But when Paul writes about a Christian's wrestling, he is out to make an emphasis by contrast
between the riots and persecutions stirred up in
the natural realm by human puppets dominated
and directed by evil powers of darkness, and the
supernatural conflict with the hosts of wicked
spirits. In 2 Corinthians 1:8 he refers to a literal
and actual flesh-and-blood situation which he
identifies as "our trouble which came to us in
Asia." It is quite possible that he is referring to the
train of events that are recorded in Acts 19. I like
to think that the things which were the ingre-
dients of what Paul calls *"our trouble"* helped him
to learn the secret of what he teaches as *"our
wrestling."* The business of war is learned in war,
in actual combat situations, not from theories
expounded or drill ground exercises. We should

beware of activities that do not bring us to grips with the enemy. Everywhere Paul went his activities stirred up the enemy and brought him into action like a roaring lion. In Ephesus Paul was hit by troubles that caused him to despair even of life itself. So he was anxious for the friends there to have the right perspective and a clear comprehension of the relationship between *"our trouble"* and *"our wrestling."*

The Christians at Ephesus could easily have seen the warfare only as a physical threat from the bloodthirsty silversmith's union under Demetrius. Or, they could have thought of the trouble as a conflict between Christianity and local culture. To correct these very natural ideas, Paul turns their minds from the human causes and introduces them to the real source of the trouble—"principalities, authorities, world rulers of the darkness, and spiritual forces of wickedness." The attacks that are physical and come against us through our circumstances are only the symptoms of the very real hostility of the world rulers of the darkness under the prince of the power of the air. Our first call is to withstand these invisible enemies. But how can mere humans grapple with and drive back invisible and intangible supernatural forces in the heavenlies? Paul takes great pains to give a full and complete answer.

The climax that the apostle makes in his letter to the Ephesians could startle us out of our complacency were we to follow the general practice of

readers of fiction. They like to look ahead to the
end of the story to see what the ending is going to
be. As far as Paul is concerned, all the exciting
things happen at the beginning of his letter. But
this is no cause for us to treat the end as if it were
an anticlimax and proceed to forget it. On the
contrary, the wealth of stacked-up truth is specifi-
cally spelled out to prepare us for the grand climax
in chapter 6, where our confrontation with the
arrayed supernatural powers under Satan is set
before us as the logical conclusion. This is what it
is all about. Our wrestling does not begin in our
hearts. It has as its foundation the mighty victory
over Satan that Jesus Christ won on the Cross—
and then all that God did with Him as the direct
result of that victory and also with us when God
gave Him to be "Head over all things to the
Church," His Body. The exaltation of the Head
"far above all rule, and authority, and power, and
dominion . . ." (Eph. 1:21 ASV), far from separating Him from His Body on earth, has taken us in
Him as co-sharers in all that God has done with
Him, so that we are "seated together with Him in
heavenly places."

So when Paul says, "In conclusion, strengthen
yourself always in the Lord and in the energy of
His might" (Eph. 6:10–Moule), his finger is pointing back to the foundational truths he has developed earlier. Satan is a defeated foe, with a
crushed head. There is no power in him, nor are
there any means available to him to reach and

unseat the Victor of Calvary now seated at the right hand of the Father. This is one fact that we need to keep strengthening ourselves with. And there is another: All the things that God did for the Head, He did for the Body also. This means that positionally we are in the heavenlies in our Head. Our strengthening in the Lord is achieved as we reckon by faith on what God has told us that He has done in fact. "The true order of faith," says Dr. Stuart Holden, "is not that we have to live an earthly life with a view to heaven, but that we are called to a heavenly life with a view to earth." Oh, that all believers could realize and appropriate continually for themselves by faith the glory of the objective facts that God has told us about in His Word, and be strengthened by them, developing spiritual muscle in order to fulfill their high calling! Even though our feet are walking about here on earth, positionally our life is "hid with Christ in God." So we go into battle not from the perspective of our circumstances here on earth, but from our position above in Christ.

This position of ours is not some terrific Mt. Everest that we are required to mount in our own strength. God has already placed us at the top in our unassailable Head, in order that by virtue of this position His will might be done down here on earth as it is in heaven through His believers. It is not for us to fight *for* victory, because "we are more than conquerors through Him that loved us." Our fight is *from* victory; and from this vantage point, empowered with Christ's might, and completely enclosed in the whole armor of God, the powers of evil are compelled to back off as we resist them.

As Paul develops the concept of conflict against "the spiritual forces of wickedness in the heavenly places" (Eph. 6:12), the conflict words that he emphasizes are *"withstand"* and *"stand."* Our defense armor guarantees total security when it is put on with prayer—for, in essence, the girdle, breastplate, helmet, shoes and shield are Jesus Christ. In Him we are complete. The repeated emphasis on "stand" and "withstand" and, in the epistles of James and Peter, on "resist" suggests that the Christian's danger and the devil's advantage lie in the believer's relinquishing his position and attempting to tackle some problem from the human, flesh-and-blood level. To get the Christian to react this way, the devil blows up a storm on the lake or a riot or the wild beasts at Ephesus and thus stimulates in us a panic to act according to the immediate predicament we are in without taking time to lay hold of the objective facts of God's promises. The devil is a panic artist and plays heavily on our self-consciousness in emergency situations. J. O. Fraser puts it this way:

> Each time your spirit goes under and faints in the trials which come to you, you lose mastery over the powers of darkness—i.e., you get below them instead of abiding above them in God. Every time you take the earth standpoint, you take a

place below the powers of darkness. The mastery of them depends on your spirit's abiding in the place above them, and the place above them means knowing God's outlook, God's thought, God's plan, God's ways, by abiding with Christ in God.

4

Dealing with the Enemy in Society

Our generation has eyed with increasing trepidation the successive waves of evil which have infiltrated world society. The foundations of morality are being undermined. The central influences of life are being taken over by men from the bottom levels of society in contrast to earlier generations. God's authority in society is mediated from the top in the punishing of evil and the rewarding of good. But when control is taken over by the men at the bottom, we may be sure that the devil is in it. Thus permissiveness and situation ethics have blurred the issues, weakened the power to discern evil under its camouflage of misrepresentation, and then sapped the will to resist. Religious heretical sects are multiplying and gaining power. Drugs that blow the mind have taken captive many of the upcoming generation. Enemy attack has brought its casualties in every part of corporate life—the family, the educational system, the judicial system, and even the church. The pattern is to compromise or to break away from God's fixed moral standards.

What all this is saying is that, the "principalities and powers in heavenly places," have mustered their unseen array, rigged their Trojan horse, infiltrated society, and opened the gates for a flood of evil to take over.

The Bible has alerted us to the possibility of supernatural evil powers establishing themselves in local cultures and then controlling life and custom. The messenger of the church at Pergamos is reminded of the grim fact that he dwells "where Satan's seat is." The obvious implication of this is that Satan's infiltration had reached its intended climax in the establishment of a control center on earth, from which to direct the powers of darkness in their opposition to God's purposes of grace.

Questions again flood our minds. How do these spirit powers exert their influence in society? Where do they get in? Is there a distinctive *modus operandi* that would help us identify them? What can or what should we be doing to control and prevent their intrusion? Since God is sovereign and omnipotent, is it not our place to let Him deal with these supernatural powers in His own time and way?

The Bible must have answers to these questions, and it does. But the terrifying fact of a hostile world of evil and malicious spirits paralyzes many Christians into inactivity and unwillingness to seek out Biblical answers and to apply them. Edith Schaeffer says that "there is a deafness, a blindness, an insensitivity among many Christians, for they refuse to recognize the war in which they are involved. They are letting the enemy attack and score victories without resistance."

There are many clear indications of Satan's motives and methods given us in the Bible, if only we would heed them. He is the arch-deceiver, adversary, accuser, the father of lies, and a "murderer from the beginning." His central purpose is to pull God from His throne in the minds of men and to take that throne himself. To do this, he scored a flying start over the whole human race through our forefather Adam. Having won Adam over to his side, his fight is to maintain his advantage over mankind. To do this, he has his control centers run by men who have rejected God's control, the world's strong natural leaders who want to shape history after their own ideals; and in smaller communities the witch doctors, and leaders in heretical sects. We have a good example of this in the worship of the goddess Artemis (Diana, KJV). In modern history, ancestor worship in China and Japan are other examples. On the other side, the Christian must make the reconquest of the ground yielded to the devil his invariable study and be committed to the goals of his Captain.

However, what we are seeing today is the sacrificing of the localized culture controls. The once powerful lama system of Tibet has been completely broken up in order to bring the Tibetans into the larger orbit of atheistic communism. Thus some of the centuries-old cultures are being forced to yield to the mold of one great anti-God system, so the devil's strong natural leader will have a unified world under his control. Satan is realizing that time is beyond his control and is running out on him. This multiplies his fury, especially as he realizes how limited is his success in welding the nations together. He seems to have more success in fragmenting Christians than he does in uniting his own side.

It seems to me that the shuffling of loyalties among the nations of the world's unholy alliances is evidence of God's working to scatter and confuse rebellious elements as He did at the Tower of Babel. This in itself is a guide for us as we pray for "kings and all in authority." We would see these things if we were watching unto prayer. We miss them because we confine our living and interest to earth and ignore our responsibilities in the heavenlies. We have the man's-eye view, instead of communing long and deeply with the Lord to get the Lord's-eye view. Should we not encourage each other to gain imperial perspective in our praying?

We look out on wars and rumors of war, political and economic instability, visa limitations on missionaries in some countries, and every kind of obstacle put in the way of the Church to prevent her from fulfilling her commission. And how do we react to these things? Yes, we do go to prayer, but generally our praying centers around the

missionary and ignores the powers that arrange
these things. Consequently our praying, like King
Canute's command to the waves to come no
further up the beach, does nothing. Barriers are
not moved by God's omnipotence until the
believer takes the initiative and stands his ground
in the heavenly places to engage the powers of
evil that are directly the cause of the ground-level
troubles, and resists them in the name of the
Victor of Calvary.

What does Paul do in the scary situation at
Ephesus? He gets together with Gaius and Aristar-
chus, or whoever was available, and together they
take their position in Christ in the heavenlies and
wrestle with and withstand the powers of evil that
are manipulating the willing puppets on the
streets. Immediately there is a break in the situation. Empowered in the Lord and in the strength
of His might and panoplied in heavenly armor,
they force Satan to yield ground, and the town
clerk quietens the screaming mob.

Such resistance against supernatural powers is
not done boastfully or presumptuously, but
humbly as befits those who realize that they have
no might in themselves and that they owe everything to the grace and power of God. The exercise
is not a call for self-advertisement as some would
make it. It is the ordained function of those who
are in Christ and, I think we should add, of those
who are filled with the Spirit. God does not
commission men not filled with the Spirit to fight

His battles. Paul was filled with the Holy Spirit when he confronted Elymas the sorcerer and exposed the devil's attack and defeated him (Acts 13:9). It is not to be passed over that the command to be filled with the Spirit comes in the context of the Christian's walk on earth and his warfare in the heavenlies.

5

Rendering the Enemy Powerless

The vocabulary of attack is not popular today. Many of the Lord's eagles have been influenced by the mood of the world and have assumed the character of doves. So there is a need for prayer eagles who will mount up in the full assurance of faith that they are indeed "seated with Christ in the heavenlies," and then from this position move to resist the enemy and overcome him by the blood of the Lamb, and the word of their testimony in the power of the Spirit of God.

J. O. Fraser, pioneer missionary to the Lisu tribe in Southwest China with the China Inland Mission, experienced how intense the wrestling with the powers of darkness can be before the "strong man" is finally forced to yield up his prey. Here is an account of his soul travail as told by Mrs. Howard Taylor, in *Behind the Ranges:*

> Strange uncertainty began to shadow his inward life. All he had believed and rejoiced in became unreal, and even his prayers seemed to mock him as the answers faded into nothing-

ness. . . . In his solitude, depression such as he had
never known before closed down on him. . . .
Deeply were the foundations shaken in those days
and nights of conflict, until Fraser realized that
behind it all were "powers of darkness," seeking
to overwhelm him. He dared to invade Satan's
kingdom, undisputed for ages. At first, vengeance
had fallen on the Lisu inquirers, an easy prey.
Now, he himself was attacked—and it was war to
the death, spiritually.

It was at this stage, when he was tempted to end
everything, that a magazine came in the mail.
Eagerly he read and reread every word until the
truth of the Word of God gripped him and set him
free. This is how he himself describes what went
on in his heart during those days:

> What it showed me was that deliverance from
> the power of the evil one comes through definite
> resistance on the ground of the Cross. I am an
> engineer and believe in things working. . . . The
> passive side of leaving everything to the Lord
> Jesus as our life, while blessedly true, was not all
> that was needed just then. Definite resistance on
> the ground of the Cross was what brought me
> light. For I found that it worked. . . . The cloud of
> depression dispersed. I found that I could have
> victory in the spiritual realm whenever I wanted
> it. The Lord Himself resisted Satan vocally: "Get
> thee behind me, Satan!" I, in humble dependence
> on Him, did the same. I talked to Satan at that
> time, using the promises of Scripture as weapons.
> And they worked.

We are often so familiar with the truth of Scripture that we lose the sense of its practicality. The

redemptive purposes of God move to their fruition by way of the Incarnation. So today the same principle applies. God has chosen us for the present as well as for the future. We are chosen for "good works that God hath foreordained that we should walk in them." And part of that has to be in activities that bring us into close touch with His enemy, frightful and repulsive though that may seem. We have been conditioned to a more comfortable form of Christianity, and it may take some wrestling on God's part before we are ready to give up and cast our dreams of ease away. One of the main purposes in the Incarnation of Jesus Christ was to "render powerless him that had the power of death, that is, the devil" (Heb. 2:14). The only way the devil can be rendered powerless today is as the truth and reality of the Savior's victory through His death on the Cross is administered by the believer on earth operating in the Name of the Lord Jesus Christ. The truth of this is shown in the testimony of the Lord Himself when the seventy He had sent out returned to render an account of their ministry. Jesus said then, "I beheld Satan as lightning fall from heaven" (Luke 10:18). Because our activity in prayer and service does not bring us into close touch with the enemy, the experience of the disciples, which should be ours, is rarely experienced.

Again J. O. Fraser can help us to understand the implications of this teaching from his actual experiences with the Lisu tribe in Southwest China. This is what he says:

Satan's tactics seem to be as follows: He will first of all oppose our breaking through to the place of a real living faith, by all means in his power. He detests the prayer of faith, for it is an authoritative "notice to quit." We often have to strive and wrestle in prayer before we attain this quiet, restful faith. And until we break right through and *join hands with God* we have not attained to real faith at all. However, once we attain to a real faith, all the forces of hell are impotent to annul it. The real battle begins when the prayer of faith has been offered.

6

Long-Range Penetration

*Let the reconquest of enemy-held
territory be our invariable study.*

One of the stratagems of war is to infiltrate
specially trained and equipped forces behind the
front line of the attacking enemy in order to
disrupt his support systems and thus weaken his
offensive thrust. The devil is no slouch when it
comes to finding new and tricky ways for reduc-
ing the effectiveness of the thrust of God's Church
in the world. So we may be sure that there is
nothing that he does not know about infiltration.

During the period of the Vietnam war there was
a lot of bitterness and controversy at home. Many
of the young people who were eligible for the
draft, with their loved ones, were infected with
the anti-overseas-involvement complex. As I read
the signs of the times, it seems to me that this same
anti-overseas-involvement complex was shifted
cleverly over into the thinking of Christian young
people in churches and Bible schools and semi-
naries as Satan's infiltration strategy. Once they
were gripped by the bug, the suggestion that it

was God's command to go into all the world and preach the Gospel to every creature was quickly shot down. By infiltrating behind the Church's attacking front into the area where the supporting power of the main offensives were centered and sabotaging the attack potential of the Church by discrediting the cause and rationale of overseas missions, the devil had gained some ground for his side. The number of those willing to consider going overseas to reinforce the front lines spearhead was cut quite measurably.

In modern warfare infiltration is now accepted as standard procedure and is universally practiced. In World War II one who contributed largely to bolder developments of this particular strategy was Major General Orde Wingate, a man who in extraordinary measure was motivated to carry the fight to the enemy. Because of his reputation in this type of warfare and his experience in Ethiopia and Israel, he was sent for when the situation in Burma was threatening, following the retreat from Rangoon. For the reconquest of territory overrun by the enemy, Wingate formed the Long-Range Penetration Group (LRP), and organized an expedition to penetrate behind the enemy lines and operate there as a part of the main offensive. With their special training and equipment, and relying on supply drops from the air, these brigades were to ambush the enemy's support columns, blow up his supply dumps, and strangle his lifeline to the front-line troops.

The effectiveness of Wingate's Chindits, as they

were called, is better gauged from the testimony of the enemy than from many of his fellow-officers, who doubted that any good was accomplished. This is what one Japanese officer wrote: "How was it that we Japanese were so triumphant in the beginning and had to endure failure in the end? What happened in Burma? In coming to any conclusion, we must not forget Major General Orde Wingate. . . . He reduced the Japanese power to wage war on four Burma fronts and so fatally affected the balance."[1] After Wingate's death in a plane crash it was said of him that "he had discovered a strange and perilous path which only the bravest could follow, but victory was at its end."[2]

During World War II I was attached to a military mission in India. As circumstances forced this unit to be disbanded, its personnel were up for grabs by special force groups. I volunteered to Force 136, a special force that operated as a long-range penetration force in Burma and Malaya. This is where my interest in long-range penetration began. I am now sure that the LRP principle is something that applies as well to the warfare of the Christian soldier as it did for Wingate's Chindits in Burma. The authority and the brains behind an attack always come from the commander-in-chief at the rear. So we may be sure that behind the assaults of the enemy seen in local situations is the authority of Satan and his world rulers of the darkness.

The pioneer of long-range penetration in God's army has to be Moses. In Exodus 17 Israel is attacked by a marauding band of Amalekites. In this case it required a two-fold thrust to defeat the desert marauders. Joshua, the commander-in-chief of Israel's army, is sent out to fight against the enemy, whose obvious purpose is to deny the hosts of Israel the right to the water that God had caused to flow for His people. They wanted that water for themselves and resented the presence of God's people in their territory. But even as Moses commissions Joshua to select his troops for the battle, he has in mind the lessons God has been teaching him in Egypt and at the Red Sea. Moses realizes that the rod in his hand is not just a shepherd's staff. It is "the rod of God," and the man that has that rod carries the symbol of God's delegated authority.

Up to this point in his experience God has always instructed Moses with regard to whatever it is that God wants to do when he stretches out the rod. But here for the first time Moses has no instructions from God. For the first time he moves to exercise that delegated authority with no specific instructions from Him. He has learned his lesson. When God's people are under attack, it is the responsibility of the man with God's delegated authority to exercise that authority in God's name. In this case the rod is not stretched out to bring on some physical phenomena, but to resist the principalities and powers and the hosts of wicked spirits that are responsible for the Amalekite attack. So Moses climbs the hill, which is a counterpart action to that of the believer who takes his stand in his position in Christ "far above all principality, and power, and might, and dominion." He is not just escaping from the danger zone in order to pray for Joshua and his soldiers, as some would claim; he has a vital role to fulfill. From his vantage-point he exercises the authority of the "stronger than the strong" and binds the power of the "strong man" armed. By resisting the enemy at his most vulnerable point, Joshua is able to drive off the flesh-and-blood enemy, who lose their will and power to fight.

There are two aspects of prayer that we need to take a closer look at. One is illustrated for us in Philippians 1:19, where Paul says this: "For I (the missionary at the front line) know that this (situation that I am in) shall turn to my salvation through your prayer and the supply of the Spirit of Jesus Christ." Paul is the main spearhead of missionary attack for His Lord. But even though he has achieved his objective in reaching an almost lifetime goal, he is bound and held in a Roman prison. In this situation he is bursting with praise as he realizes that the prayers of his friends at Philippi are channeling the supply of the Spirit of his conquering Lord into his situation. And it is this fact of supporting prayer that is turning apparent loss into stepping-stones for the furtherance of the Gospel. The Church at Philippi is part and parcel of the main offensive. It is their responsibility to see that the necessary supplies get through to their brave soldier at the front. Faithfully they devote themselves to their mission, so that Paul is able to record victories even though he is chained and unable to go out preaching.

But there is another aspect of prayer that has a completely different approach and function, and yet is a vital, though often neglected, part of the main offensive of God's missionary program. This aspect is put before us in the words of the Lord Jesus, "How can one enter into a strong man's house, and spoil his goods?" (Matt. 12:29). Victory can be hastened and casualties lessened by infiltrating into the enemy's vulnerable control zone, where plans for attack are conceived and from which the orders are issued. This area is not marked on our atlases as a geographic point, but that does not make it any less real. To the believer the heavenlies are more real than the temporal things of earth. Satan's control zone is vulnerable, because he is a defeated foe. Christ crushed his head for him at Calvary, and that victory means that every believer who holds his position in Christ by faith is co-sharer in the triumph of that mighty act. The devil must yield ground before the believer who resists him with the delegated authority of the "stronger than the strong."

Jesus had another word for us: He says, "Whatsoever ye shall bind on earth shall be bound in heaven" (Matt. 18:18). The initiative for taking action is placed on the Church with the promise that heaven will endorse that initiative. The temerity of this aspect of prayer warfare appalls

many and, because the results are not easily
measured, is often put to one side. But it is a way of
victory.

Many of General Wingate's fellow officers
played down what he was doing and rated him
impossible, unorthodox, anti-authority, and mad.
But not the men that were under him and committed to his leadership. One of his column leaders
makes this comment:

> To those who took part in it, the Wingate expedi-
> tion was a watershed in their lives. Before it, one's
> appreciation of values was only half developed.
> Now we have new standards and new touch-
> stones.[3]

In my own experience long-range penetration
in prayer has been a watershed, and I now realize
that my earlier appreciation of prayer values was
only half developed. But there are cautions that
need to be sounded. The enemy against us is a real
person, and he is spirit; therefore at no time dare
we move against him or any of his wicked spirits
with weapons that are not spiritual, and then only
under the leading of the Spirit of God. In this
warfare it is not for us to pick and choose at will
where we think we should attack. We must be first
submissive to God. That is the order of priority
James gives us, "Submit yourselves to God. Resist
the devil, and he will flee from you" (James 4:7).

Recently a burden was placed on my heart for
two specific areas in Southeast Asia. The enemy
was staging strong opposition to the progress of
the Gospel, and it was borne in on me that God

was waiting for someone to resist the devil. The burden persisted; so asserting my position with Christ in the heavenlies on the basis of God's Word and strengthened with His might, I took unto me the whole armor of God in order to stand against the wiles of the devil and to withstand his opposition to the Gospel. Some time passed and then the news from the missionaries in both those places began to change. The resisting powers in both cases were weakened, making possible victories for the Lord. I would never mention this, but so many are shy of this kind of warfare and need a definite example to guide them; so for that reason alone I have included this personal testimony.

On the last day before General Wingate's expedition crossed the Chindwin and entered enemy-held territory, he issued his battle order of the day. It included this sentence:

> Finally, knowing the vanity of man's effort and the confusion of his purpose, let us pray that God may accept our services and direct our endeavors, so that when we have done all, we may see the fruit of our labors and be satisfied.[4]

How like Paul's battle order of the day in Ephesians 6!—

> Finally, my brethren, let your hearts be strengthened in the Lord, and in the conquering power of His might. Put on the whole armor of God, that you may be able to stand firm against the wiles of the devil. For the adversaries with whom we wrestle are not flesh and blood, but they are the principalities, the powers, and the sovereigns of this present darkness, the spirits of

evil in the heavens. Wherefore, take up with you to the battle the whole armor of God, that you may be able to withstand them in the evil day, and, having overthrown them all, to stand unshaken (Eph. 6:10–13).

And Moses' battle orders in Exodus 17:9—

Choose us out men, and go out, fight with Amalek: tomorrow I will stand on the top of the hill with the rod of God in mine hand.

1 Major General Derek Tulloch, *Wingate in Peace and War*, History Book Club, 1972.
2 *Ibid.*
3 Bernard Fergusson, *Beyond the Chindwin*, Collins, 1945.
4 *Ibid.*

7

Slackened Bowstrings

It was said of the late Sir Winston Churchill that "he mobilized the English language and sent it into battle." The sagacity and satire, the zesty wit and daring defiance of this great man fired the inspiration of his generation to fight for victory. In his orders to Lord Louis Mountbatten, Churchill said this: "You are to plan for the offensive. In your headquarters you will never think defensively."

What Sir Winston did for the English language the Apostle Paul has done for the language of some of his letters, particularly Ephesians and 2 Timothy. Paul seems to have had more opportunity to appreciate the significance of the sacrifice involved in the calling of the soldier than the other writers of the New Testament. To the timely arrival of the Roman centurion and his troops Paul owed his life when a fanatical mob was determined to wipe him out. A strong military escort conveyed him by night to the security of the garrison headquarters in Caesarea. And there for two years he had the range of the barracks and lived among the soldiers. But it was in Rome that the links of his close attachment to soldiers were forged—in the chain that secured him around the clock to members of the Imperial Guard. In the intimacy of this compulsory relationship Paul would hear tales of bitter battles, sufferings and hardships of every description. Soldier that he was himself at heart, he found in their flesh-and-blood wars and experiences the illustration he needed of the quality and price of commitment that was the criterion of a good soldier of Jesus Christ. So after ingesting the imagery of weapons, warriors, and warfare and then mobilizing his thoughts in terms of spiritual conflict, this indefatigable soldier pours forth in battle language a letter that has inspired Christians of every generation.

But Paul's particular concern is for Timothy, his beloved son in the faith. Like a commanding officer, he is solicitous for the morale of the officers and men under him. The historic setting for the second letter seems to fit best soon after the outburst of persecution against the Christians which began when Nero set fire to Rome and then focused the suspicions of the populace onto the Christians. As Paul is dragged off to face martyrdom, he cannot erase from his memory Timothy's outburst of tears at their last parting. Through force of circumstances Timothy the leaner—weak stomach and all—is now Timothy the leader, and he needs all the stiffening and encouragement he can get. A sense of urgency to write grips the apostle as he thinks of Timothy, standing alone and unsupported as the pressure intensifies, causing "all they which are in Asia" to scurry for cover like hunted rabbits.

Like Churchill, Paul sees only one course of action—attack. He wants Timothy to face the enemy with his sword drawn and the bowstrings of his resolves taut. (Speaking of bowstrings, the word detente comes to us from the French and is derived from the idea of slackening the bowstrings that are set for attack.)

In warfare there are four possible attitudes—offense, defense, detente, and desertion. It is the first one of these attitudes that our adversary fears, for "Satan trembles when he sees the weakest saint upon his knees." He will therefore do all in his power to put God's people on the defensive or to get them to the Plain of Ono (like he tried with Nehemiah), there to talk detente or else to frighten them into deserting. I think the Lord must have chuckled in foresight when the devil, in trying to entice Nehemiah, put the right answer into his mouth for the English-speaking world by inviting him to "O no"! Satan can get along very well with Christians as long as they are on the defensive, seeking detente, or deserting. Therefore, if we are determined to see him defeated in our own hearts and in our society, we must be only and always committed to the offensive.

As the generation that Churchill spoke to was war-minded, he had things going for him. But other generations do not necessarily have the same mind about war or respond in the same way.

Take this example from Scripture: The generation of Joshua's day was committed by God's command to a war of offensive action. But after Joshua arose another generation which slackened their bowstrings and sought the civilian life of coexistence by compromise. Like others, they probably argued that war is immoral and refused to see that they were blurring the distinctions between the rights of their cause as a nation under God and the evils God was using them to exterminate. They purposefully dissolved their sense of obligation to moral objectives. And because of their slackened bowstrings, Satan had his heyday. The saints of God became characterized by the very sins that were the cause of God's offensive campaign against the Canaanites.

The attitudes of the post-Joshua generation are paralleled by a post-World War II permissive generation that aims "to do that which is right in its own eyes." The thing that we need to be afraid of today is that the spirit that produces world trends should invade Christ's mighty army and argue us off the offensive into a compromised coexistence with the world's attitudes—so that we end up just like the world, taking lessons in French and practicing detente.

A permissive society is one that faces the onslaughts of evil with relaxed bowstrings. For the Christian soldier the price of commitment to the cause of Christ is too high only when he wants less than victory. There are no safe battles—but there are no safe compromises either. The time has come to treat our enemies, all of them, as enemies. We will not win our battles by sheltering one little lust in our hearts while outwardly making a show of killing off others.

The wars of earth ebb and flow like the tides. One year they're on, and the next they go into history books. Paul's battle language says, "Our wrestling is. . . ." He does not say that it was or will be, but that it is a continuously present factor in our lives as Christians. And from this struggle there is no demobilization or discharge, at least in this life. The implacable hate and serpentine sub-tlety of our adversary the devil demands of Christ's soldiers bowstrings taut to the gates of Heaven.

8

Weapons and the Will

> On the battlefield the real enemy is fear and not the bayonet and the bullet.
>
> **Robert Jackson**

Weapons do give an impressiveness to the soldier on the parade ground. But as soldiers facing an implacable foe, we have to realize that battles are won only by the soldier who fights, and fighting involves using a weapon. Unused weapons do not inflict casualties on the enemy nor win wars. Therefore the ability and the will to use weapons is what warfare is all about. It is not enough to give mental assent to the fact that a spiritual warfare is going on. Passivity towards our enemy is what the devil wants from us and is his trick to cool the ardor of God's men of war. There is no neutrality on the battlefield. Jesus said, "He that is not with Me is against Me." Everywhere the Word of God is against passivity and advocating action: "Fight the good fight of faith. . . ." "Endure hardness as a good soldier. . . ." "Resist the devil. . . ." "Take the sword of the Spirit. . . ."

There is one thing that we do need to consider, and that is the will of the soldier to use his weapon in actual combat situations. The trained capabilities and skill of the soldier in hitting the bull's-eye on the practice range is not enough. To illustrate what I mean, let me quote from the book, *Men Against Fire*, by S. L. A. Marshall:

> Only five infantry companies [on Omaha Beachhead, June 6, 1944] were tactically effective. In these companies one-fifth of the men fired their weapons during the day-long advance from the water's edge to the first row of villages—a total of not more than 450 men firing consistently.

On another front the survey turned up these facts:

> The best showing that could be made by the most spirited and aggressive companies was that one man in four had made some use of his fire power.

So it is from facts like these that we draw the conclusion that having a weapon and having the will to use that weapon are not the same thing.

Saul, Israel's commander-in-chief, towers head and shoulders above the rest of the army. Confronting him across the valley is the Philistine army. Daily their champion, Goliath, struts out to belittle Saul's army and to berate Israel's God. Meanwhile, Saul sits in his tent like a prisoner in his cell and broods over his dire predicament. Yet all the while, in the corner of the tent, lie his armor and weapons. He's happy enough for some-

one else to use them, but as far as he is concerned
his will is frozen, and nothing will change his
thinking.

> *'Tis man's perdition to be safe,*
> *When for truth he ought to die.*
>
> **Emerson**

Saul would have liked to have the chance to
choose his own problems. And wouldn't we all?
But life does not grant us that luxury. Only the
arrival of David, the youthful shepherd, changes
the situation in the army camp and causes a ray of
hope to shimmer in the gloom. His sling may seem
unrealistic and inadequate in contrast to the sheer
weight of Goliath's armor and weapons. The odds
may be heavily weighted against him. Even his
older brothers scorn and abuse him. But David's
warrior-heart is pounding insistently as he listens
to the abuse of the Philistine giant against the God
he loves and who has helped him in his past
battles with lion and bear. With God's honor at
stake, he is perfectly willing to lay his own life on
the line to provide God with an opportunity to
vindicate His name before the heathen and His
own people. Yes! God needed a victory, but only
as some man is willing to use his weapon can
victory become a reality. And since none of the
soldiers in Saul's army are volunteering for the
privilege, David wills that this shall be his battle,
but only as God's representative to fight on His
behalf. God needs the will of men to take up

weapons and engage the enemy. When He has such a man, the deadlock is broken immediately and the victory is God's.

Once again Saul is in trouble. This time the Philistines have hemmed him in, and most of his army has deserted him. So he has another awkward situation dumped onto his plate. He would have liked nothing better than to be able to dispense with the next item on the agenda. He is so absorbed with his own plight that he has no time nor inclination to concern himself with God's honor. So again someone else has to handle the problem. Jonathan, like his friend David, is burdened for God's honor in the situation and is prepared to lay his life on the line and trust God for a victory. Thus alone, except for his armor-bearer, he ventures forward and attacks the enemy garrison. When God sees a weapon being used in His name and faith daring to attempt the impossible, He musters Heaven's cohorts and moves in to confound and rout the enemy.

The lesson we learn from these two incidents of David and Jonathan is that victory comes to God's side only when a man wills to use his weapon in direct confrontation with the enemy. The opportunity for God is closed until the will of a man opens it by determining to use his weapon. The New Testament principle backs this up. Jesus said, "Whatsoever ye shall bind on earth shall be bound in heaven" (Matt. 18:18). Jesus puts the initiative for action into the hands of His people and promises that when they act, Heaven will endorse.

In the warfare of the Church on earth, it seems to me that the number of those using their weapons is on a par with the World War II statistics just quoted. We sing, "Like a mighty army, moves the Church of God . . .," but if only one out of four in our evangelical churches is using his weapons, our attitude gives the lie to our profession. If three-fourths of those on church membership rolls are so uncertain and confused about their role in the conflict or so paralyzed by fear that they do not use their weapons, then victory will obviously be that much longer in coming. "The Gospel moves at a slow and timid pace when the saints are not at their prayers early and late and long."

The will to use weapons when under attack is derived from inner attitudes of the heart. When our own personal problems fill the horizon, it is more likely that depression, morbidity, and passivity will cause us to withdraw to our inner mental monastery, where we can shut out the realities of life and brood on the impossibilities in our situation, letting victory go by default to the enemy. That surely has to be one of the lessons that we learn from Saul's behavior.

Many are aware of inner defeat, but do not know how to handle it. They lack the knowledge of how to apply spiritual resources which are available to them for the problem. Or, it could be that they lack the will to apply those resources to their particular area of need through fear of the exposure that will be involved. This attitude plays havoc with the emotions and manifests itself in resentment, depression, and withdrawal. In their hearts they want to do the right thing and sincerely desire God's will, but the trouble is that desire by itself is powerless against the enemy unless followed by the will to act. Basic to all victory over the devil is the unashamed use of the Word of God and the application of its absolute and objective truth and promises in a direct confrontation against the lies, deceits, and misquotes of the devil. Satan cannot face the Word of God thrust at him by the believing heart in the power of the Spirit.

The ground of a believer's faith is the objective truth of the Gospel, which lays down the unalterable and unassailable facts of his position: "Our life is hid with Christ in God. . . ." "God . . . hath raised us up together, and made us sit together in heavenly places in Christ Jesus." But, like Saul, many have the armor stashed away in the corner of the tent and are seeking after some experience that will appeal to their senses as being more evidently real and tangible than the bare objective facts stated in God's Word. To feel something tempts them into thinking that experience is more convincing to their inner assurance than faith, which has only the Word to rest on. A person in this frame of mind focuses on his condition rather than his position and is easy meat for the "roaring lion."

The subjective feelings of the individual, his sense of guilt and failure, his emotional distress

can find release from inner recriminations only as
faith takes its stand on the believer's God-given
position as God has stated it. This position, unlike
our condition, is not subject to ups and downs and
is not affected by ebb and flow tides as our
emotions are. We are accepted in Christ, and since
nothing is needed to enhance or improve His
acceptance, we need to put our feet firmly on this
fact that God has stated. This does not mean that
we condone failure—far from it! What it does
mean is that we cease to live only at the level of
our feelings and begin to appropriate by active
faith the objective facts that God has given us in
His sure Word. This is our only sure ground for
resisting the devil. The sword of the Spirit is there,
but we need the will to take it. The Christian
soldier who allows his mind to be filled with his
troubled condition and withdraws from the
conflict into his mental monastery, ceases to be a
part of God's solution to the problem and becomes
instead a part of the problem. So from the
Captain's viewpoint a sizable number of His fighting forces are only statistics that are tied up with
their inner attitudes that inhibit them from active
participation in resisting the enemy.

This lack of will on the part of God's soldiers is
taken up in the song of Deborah and Barak (Jud.
5). It is one thing to be so paralyzed by fear and
confusion in combat that the soldier fails to use his
weapon. In that case there is at least the plus factor
of his presence alongside his buddies that keeps
the morale from completely crumbling. But to stay

at home minding the sheep like Reuben and not be involved at all is sin. It is to these that the angel of the Lord speaks and says, "Curse ye Meroz . . . because they came not to the help of the Lord . . ." (Jud. 5:23). God does not act independently of His people. His opportunity comes when His faithful ones will and determine to use their weapons against His enemies.

PRAYER:

Dear Father! I confess that often fear, ignorance, indecision, or sometimes just sheer laziness have earned for me the curse of Meroz. I have not gone to the help of the Lord against His enemies, but have stayed at home. For this sin, I ask Your forgiveness. And, since I must fight if I would reign, increase my courage, Lord.

9

Peace Through Victory

Old Testament examples of prayer at work portray most dramatically for us the believer's authority over all the power of God's enemies. There is a finality that will not be gainsaid in the way the superior strength of alien armies is disposed of as God's servants pray.

This finality is not seen in the political bargaining that characterizes our day. Compromises are made, peace treaties are signed, and the peacemakers move to other danger spots; but the fighting still goes on. Are we allowing our disillusionment with the world's acclaimed peacemakers to influence our thinking on spiritual warfare? Are we really convinced that our call is to spiritual welfare and peace through victory?

In any situation where Satan dominates and threatens, God looks for a man through whom He may declare war on the enemy. He purposes that through this man Satan be served notice to back up, pack up, and clear out. The power of spiritual weapons applied by insistent faith on conflict conditions cannot but thwart the enemy, bring victory to God's people, and fulfill His purposes.

This is the only explanation I have for these words from I Samuel 7:13: "So the Philistines were subdued (that is victory), and they came no more into the coast of Israel (that is victory maintained), and the hand of the Lord was against the Philistines all the days of Samuel" (that is a plus factor only to be accounted for on the basis of an intercessor at work). And there are grounds for making that conclusion: The prayer burden of Samuel's life was, "God forbid that I should sin in ceasing to pray for you."

It is the man who prays who exercises supremacy even over international situations. Men are going to have to acknowledge that peace will not be brought about through politicians, but through the intercessor who has learned to wage spiritual warfare and wins peace through victory over the principalities and powers in high places.

The life of Samuel is introduced to us in a context of prayer that works. He owed his existence first to supernatural factors, second to biological laws. The Lord had shut up Hannah's child-bearing potential. But the power of Hannah's prayer moved God to lift His restraints. She bore a son, and in triumphant testimony to the world that her prayer had brought God's supernatural response, "she called his name Samuel saying, because I asked him of the Lord."

God's contact with Samuel is on a homey, inti-

mate level. Moses climbs Mt. Sinai into the terrifying thunderings that accompany the divine
Presence. In contrast, Samuel is wakened from his
innocent childhood slumbers by the still, small
voice of God calling him. On another occasion
God steals up on him, uncovers his ear, and
delivers His message (1 Samuel 9:15, ASV marg.).
It was Samuel as God's prophet who anointed
Israel's first two kings, Saul and David. As judge,
he spent his life tramping the dusty roads of his
circuit between Ramah, Bethel, Gilgal, and
Mizpeh. In between he found time to organize the
kingdom and explain it to the people and then as
author to write it in a book and lay it up before the
Lord.

The importance of the man, however, is not
graded by his competence in any of these minis-
tries. Above and beyond the mundane things of
time and sense, he was a prayer warrior. It is in
this character that he blazes out as a star of first
magnitude. The Psalmist says: "Moses and Aaron
were among his priests, Samuel also was among
those who called on his name. They cried to the
Lord, and He answered them" (Psa. 99:6).

First Samuel 7 introduces Samuel's prayer role
in God's book of wars. The story divides easily
into three parts:

There is CLEANUP, first of all. Samuel stirs up
an old-fashioned revival meeting, urging the
people to seek the Lord in true repentance and
destroy the Baalim and the gang of female Ashta-

roth. Israel responds in brokenness and contrition.

Following the cleanup comes CRISIS. A sinister threat is concealed by the dust clouds to the west. The Philistine armies are crowding forward, bent on booty and bloodshed. And behind this crisis stands Satan. As long as Israel is kowtowing to strange gods, the people are Satan's slaves. Operation Cleanup signals rebellion from his authority. This the evil one resents. By goading his Philistine wardogs to attack, he plans to recapture his control.

Put yourself in Samuel's place. The cleanup is being challenged. A very literal foe is threatening. Caught up in a strong emotional urge of shame and contrition, the Israelites are in no condition to cope with this crisis. The threat from the advancing Philistine hordes is pressing on one side; on the other, the panic of the people. The immediate future of two nations is in Samuel's hands, and God's honor is involved. Immediate, drastic action is called for, and this is neither the time nor the place to experiment. It all rests on him for stage three.

The CLIMAX. What does Samuel do? How does he react to this crisis?" And Samuel took a sucking lamb and offered it. . . ." Sit down and think that one through! His mind may have flipped back to the slain animal in Eden's garden or to the Passover lamb, but the essentiality of his act was to point down history's road to Calvary's Lamb and the grand climax announcement: "The accuser is cast down . . . and they overcame him by the blood of the Lamb. . ." (Rev. 12:10–11).

Standing identified with the complete acceptance of his lamb, Samuel cries unto the Lord for Israel. The Lord thunders from heaven, the Philistines are frightened off, and, according to the record, "came no more into the coast of Israel."

The victory was necessary to the peace. Peace is victory sustained. The only man who can keep the enemy at bay is the intercessor, and blessed is that intercessor who knows how to use the power of the blood in spiritual warfare.

> *Precious blood, by this we conquer*
> *In the fiercest fight,*
> *Sin and Satan overcoming*
> *By its might*
>
> **F. R. Havergal**

10

Measuring Our Victories

We are as victorious as we want to be. Lack of inner victory cannot be blamed on anyone but ourselves. Each man has his own measuring cup and measures out the quantity of victory he desires. Beyond that, for some perverse reason, we will not stretch ourselves.

There are some, however, that have a different spirit. What a rebuke the testimony of their warfare for Christ is to those who are content with scanty victory! One who had a strong testimony was Pastor Hsi in China. Prior to his conversion he was an avid opium smoker and a cultured Confucianist. But when he became a new creature in Christ, what a change! One of the first things he did was to take a new name for himself, in order to proclaim to the world and to the devil himself, the direction his new life was going to take. He called himself Conquerer of Demons. He wanted to express his sense of being enlisted for life in God's army in the warfare against the powers of darkness. To a man that had grown up in terror of evil spirits and known the power of sin's bondage, it took more than courage to call himself the Devil

Overcomer. It showed the reality of his faith in God and his willingness to trust in the power of the indwelling Holy Spirit to give victory over all the power of the enemy. In Christ's name he was determined to "possess his possessions" and claim all that was his of victory through the death, resurrection, and exaltation to the throne of the Lord Jesus Christ. For the sake of the Savior he now loved, he wanted his cup of victory to be filled right to the brim.

Such a man Jehoash, grandson of Israel's king Jehu, was not. His faith could only believe for a limited victory. The story of this weak and wicked king is linked to the last recorded incident in the life of Elisha, the prophet (2 Kings 13:14–19). It is the story of two sick men. Elisha is dying of a terminal illness. Sixty years have gone by since his call to succeed Elijah, and for the last forty-five of these years nothing has been heard of him. The other sick man is the king, Jehoash. He is sick with his own inner corruption and also with shame at the humiliation of Israel under Hazael, Syria's cruel king. The strategic arms limitation that had been imposed on him since the days of his father allows him no scope for retaliating and breaking free of the bondage imposed by Hazael. What can he possibly do with fifty horsemen and ten chariots? Hearing of the sickness of Elisha, he decides to visit the prophet to see if there is some way out of his dilemma. Entering the prophet's chamber, he sobs out his problem: "O my father, my father, the chariot of Israel and the horsemen thereof!"

For years Elisha has been silently watching the judgments fall on the house of Jehu, as "the Lord began to cut Israel short." And now at last the opportunity comes to him on his death-bed to teach a lesson on how victory may be won. He gives his attention to the king, but it seems as though he has barely enough strength to gasp out his instructions. "Take bow and arrows." "Open the window eastward." "Shoot." The prophet must have realized that this would be his last chance to stir the king to strive for victory for his humiliated people.

In this object lesson with the bow and arrows, we find simple victory rules that lead to an understanding of the part we must play if we are to rise above the shame of our defeats in Christian living.

I. *"Take bow and arrows."* Demonstrate your intention to fight.

Peace at any price is not the language of God's prophet. He wants to instill in the heart of the defeated king the determination to try for victory at any cost. Tears of remorse over the state of the kingdom under his leadership are not enough. How futile is much of our wailing over our defeats and over the sick state of society around us! The first step to victory is to take up our weapons with the determination to go all out for victory. The counterpart of Elisha's command, "Take bow and arrows," is in the word of the Apostle Paul, "Take the sword of the Spirit": Is there sin in your life and bitter defeat? Then take up your weapons of the Spirit and declare war. Today the message of victory is being misrepresented, cheapened, and diluted by Christians who are content with lowered standards and limited victory, because in their hearts they do not really want victory.

II. *"Put thy hand upon thy bow ... and Elisha laid his hands upon the king's hands."* Reckon on divine faithfulness.

When utter failure and impotence moves honestly to seek victory, it will find its total weakness encompassed by strength. God identifies Himself with obedient weakness. The rule for victory is, Our hand on the weapon and His hand over ours. God is saying to us in this, as He puts His mighty hand over ours, "The battle is not yours but God's." The putting of the hand to the bow is faith's reckoning on the Divine faithfulness and claiming, "The fight which I now fight, I fight in the faithfulness of the Son of God."

III. *"Open the window eastward."* Expose the place of failure and defeat.

Face the place in your heart where the proud enemy boasts his victories. Israels' foe was to the east. The rule here is that victory arrows cannot be shot through closed windows. There are hidden things we are all afraid to face up to, specific things that cannot be glossed over as weakness inherited from others. If we are to be victorious, the windows on each particular thing that defeats our attempts to live as God would have us must be opened to expose the failures of the past and present to the Hand that controls ours on the weapon. It could be that the biggest need in your life just now is to open the windows.

IV. *"Shoot, and he shot."* Put action to your faith.

The arrow in itself may seem ineffective to deal with the particular enemy that is harassing us, but the Lord claims it as His. Elisha says to the king, "The Lord's arrow of victory, even the arrow of victory over Syria." Faith that acts will bring the foe to his knees, or send him scurrying off. So far so good, the king has shot his arrow. But there is more to the lesson than that.

V. *"Take the arrows . . . Smite upon the ground."* Take the measuring cup of victory and fill it.

Obedience is the manifestation of faith's energy. The king limited his obedience: "he smote thrice and stayed." Victory over our failures is in exact proportion to the obedience of faith. The last verse of the chapter makes this clear. There it says, " Three times did Jehoash beat him, and recovered the cities of Israel." Let it be said to his shame that he didn't believe enough; so he didn't obey enough. It is what happens in the secret chamber that determines the amount of victory we have in the actual battle of life. Though there has been failure in the past, the future, by God's grace, is always redeemable.

11

The Cutting Edge

Prayer is a weapon, a mighty weapon in a terrible conflict.

Our prayers are to be a continual, conscious, earnest effort of battle, the battle against whatever is not God's will.

P. T. Forsyth

Prayer is the cutting edge of any work for God. It is not a supplemental spiritual rocket to get some well-meaning effort off the ground. Prayer is the work and the working power in any spiritual ministry. It should be the central thrust. The spiritual history of a mission or a church is written in its prayer life. The expression of corporate life is not measured in statistics, but in prayer depth. The program of preaching, teaching and serving, the goal setting, the adoption of new, twentieth-century techniques, seminars on time management and administrative procedures are all good—but effective and productive in God's economy only as they are subject to prayer.

Considering the importance God attaches to prayer for the carrying out of His purposes on earth, we must be alert and sensitive to common habits and tendencies that impair the effectiveness and blunt the cutting edge of our praying. Prayers that have blunted edges have no power of penetration, so may not get through to the Throne. Furthermore, such prayers do not have any deterent effect on the attacking enemy. As it takes a sharp edge to inflict wounds, our best endeavors ought to be concentrating on preserving a razor-sharp cutting edge.

In a day when new and exciting cutting edges are being recommended, the tendency is to be carried away with new ideas and relegate the traditional trusty weapons to a place of lesser significance or to throw them away altogether. We need to realize that God is not going to use any means of operation just because it happens to be innovative, nor because it relates to the status quo. Edith Schaeffer warns us that "it is difficult to stand against the pull of 20th century solutions." It is easy and less troublesome to go along with the contemporary mood and give priority to outward means and methods that promise to increase the effectiveness of our service and our praying, but which often do it at the expense of inner reality.

My purpose is to intensify the inner realities and to encourage God's people to derive their value systems from the direct teaching of the Word itself and then to surrender themselves to the truth as the Holy Spirit applies it and to use it in prayer. If we do this, then there can be no fear that the cutting edge will be blunt. So let us

consider prayerfully some of the attitudes and
conceptions in a prayer life that can spoil its
cutting edge.

The concept that treats prayer as if it were
merely a supplemental booster in getting some
project off the ground makes the project primary
and the prayer secondary. Prayer was never meant
to be incidental to the work of God. It is *the* work.
The powerful locomotive is more than a meshing
of wheels and shafts. In order for it to function, it
needs steam or some other equivalent as the driving power to speed it to its destination. And so in
all work for God, prayer is the working power of
all that God would do through His people. Without prayer and waiting on God for Him to reveal
His will, our well-meant attemptings may look
impressive, but they have no power to move
towards God's goals. Supplementing our self-
conceived ideas with prayer will not transpose
them into Divine purposings. Nothing of God's
will is properly and effectually executed that is
not first begun and then carried out through
prayer.

The impression that one often gets at prayer
meetings is that petition is the pivot upon which
prayer turns and that the main function of prayer
is to handle life's emergencies. Dr. Forsyth
declares, "So many of us pray because we are
driven by need rather than kindled by grace. Our
prayer is a cry rather than a hymn. It is a quest
rather than a tryst. It trembles more than it

triumphs. It asks for strength rather than exerts it." If prayer is fostered only by emergencies and is only and always just petition, then it seems to me that some very important aspects of prayer are being ignored. Prayer is more than the Church's ambulance, called out to deal with various crises after the damage has already been done. To use it only in this way is to cheapen and do despite to the deeper significance of prayer that God teaches in the Bible. To pray in an emergency is altogether right. But to pray only in an emergency cannot be right, because this limits prayer to the area of our own self-awareness in the events of life. It makes prayer a convenience, something to which we are driven by our human perspective on the crisis, but not something in which we are drawn and energized by the Holy Spirit.

Perhaps you can recollect the changes that have taken place in your own prayer life and will agree with these remarks. "In the normal course of our spiritual growth, there comes a time when the center of prayer shifts from self to God. Petition, in its narrower sense, recedes. True, it is not excluded, for nothing that touches us can be indifferent to our Father in Heaven; . . . But petition will no longer be the pivot upon which prayer turns. The true motive power will now be to get nearer to God, to know Him better, to experience His friendship, to enter more fully into His thoughts and purposes. . . . God-conscious prayer at its highest involves honest thinking and a firm resolve to bring all our problems to the searchlight of His truth and to submit all our works to the touchstone of His interests and intentions.... God-centered prayer then means to enter the world of reality."[1]

For prayer to be effectual, we must learn to look at it from its central object and not alone from its performances. Florence Allshorn says this, "Isn't the desire behind prayer to posses something more than myself, because I'm sick with self's ineffectiveness in a world so needy? The desire [is] to be possessed of something beyond myself that can use me as its channel."[2]

The central significance of prayer is not in the things that happen as results, but in the deepening intimacy and unhurried communion with God at His central throne of control in order to discover a "sense of God's need in order to call on God's help to meet that need."[3] Prayer is first a Theocentric tryst, not just an egocentric quest; yet this is often what we make of it. To quote Florence Allshorn again, "We still struggle to put Him first in a vague and limited way. I must pray till Jesus Christ hears me and gives me what I need. I am important, the great 'I.' We must not miss the great truth that I am for Him primarily. It is a soul-shaking fact that I am not looking into some far-off sky where Someone is hidden to whom I cry; ... but that He Himself has said 'There is a place by my side.' I must see from there or I will not see; I must look at things from His standpoint...."[4]

The great "I," self-surcharged to the brim, has to be emptied in order to see the purpose and function of our relationship with God from His perspective. In its purest essence prayer is the communion of the loving, trustful soul with the heavenly Father. I think we need to study the implications of these things. Prayer must start at God's end, for is not that the control center of all that happens? Therefore our relationship with Him and our attitude towards the things He allows to disturb our lives is more important than passing on information to Him. And because of this our first duty is to make sure that we are really in that lofty place by His side with the right attitude and with nothing in us to prevent Him from hearing us and us from hearing His still, small voice. It is only from that place of closest intimacy that we may learn what that will is that we are to pray will be done on earth as it is in heaven.

1 *Creative Prayer*, E. Herman
2 *The Notebooks of Florence Allshorn*, SCM Book Club, Naperville, Ill.
3 *The Weapon of Prayer*, E. M. Bounds, Baker Book House
4 *Ibid. The Notebooks of Florence Allshorn*

12

God's Will/My Will

The natural tendency is to push forward with prayers that relate only to the causes we are interested in and to the troubles and aspirations that stem from them. The fact that two wills are at work in prayer, the will of God and the will of man, makes it imperative that the two blend into one. Unless God and man in oneness blend, a stalemate occurs. Frequently our wills are taken up with *WHAT* is happening, whereas God's will is concerned with *WHY* certain things are needed. Prayer that seeks deliverance for the sake of deliverance has lost that objectivity in prayer that Jesus teaches so carefully. When Paul prayed for himself that God would remove his thorn in the flesh, God did not give him what he asked for. Instead God taught Paul a new lesson about how to handle his personal problems. He taught him to relate the fact of God to his problem and find release that way.

And this is just what we had to learn during the four years we were under the communists in Northwest China on the Tibetan border following the takeover in 1949.* There were many blunt-edged, self-centered, subjective prayers hammering at heaven's door clamoring for answers. But God was teaching us, and no school can compare with God's school of hard knocks. Mostly our prayers were stimulated by our fears and the desperate desire to escape from the hands of the communists. From our little corner on the periphery of things we were distracted by the tension of our circumstances and pressures of duress, to say nothing of the accusations that were being cooked up against us by hate-filled men. Because of all this, our praying focused on our fears, our empty cupboard, and our uncertain future. And while this is the natural impulse, that does not make it the will of God for our praying.

Our constant struggle was to pull God over to our corner of things until we learned that self-preoccupation in prayer leads to discouragement and depression and that the more our prayers turned inward on our circumstances, the more they became subject to the law of diminishing returns. We were like the disciples when they were caught in a terrible gale while Jesus lay asleep in the stern of their swamped boat. Their preoccupation spilled over in their frenzied shouts, "Master, carest Thou not that WE perish?" (emphasis mine). Their only thought was about their predicament and the Master's apparent

---

*Full story told in *Green Leaf in Drought-Time,* by Isobel Kuhn; OMF Books, 1981.

unconcern. For us there came a day when our prayers changed. Worshiping together one morning, we came to see that the story of the storm and the sleeping Savior had a lesson for us on the availability of personal faith for the emergencies of life and that there was really no need to disturb the Lord with our troubles. So as we went to prayer we said, "Sleep on Lord, for we are not going to waken You."

However, after a year of more of other strains, and realizing that nearly all the other missionaries were out of China, we lost our recklessness, and fears began to pile up again. In this predicament God taught us to pray in the spirit of the prayer of the Son," 'I delight to do Thy will, O my God,' and since You have placed us here in Communist China for some good and acceptable purpose of Yours, we joyfully abandon ourselves to stay on here as long as You need us here." We found our strength, not in dreams of escape, but in complete surrender to whatever God wanted to do with us, realizing that God's claims are absolute and that we must accept them without bargaining. When God seems to come into our lives like a sword-blade, it is only that He might separate us from ourselves and draw us to Himself. So we took the attitude expressed in this verse:

> *Come ill, come well, the Cross, the crown,*
> *The rainbow or the thunder—*
> *I fling my soul and body down*
> *For God to plough them under.*
>
> **Robert Louis Stevenson**

Later on we came across the words of Dr. George Matheson. Blind he may have been, yet how perceptive he was when he wrote:

> Thou wouldst not have me accept Thy will because I must, but because I may. Thou wouldst have me take it, not with resignation, but with joy; not with the absence of a murmur, but with a song of praise.

So instead of being chained to our circumstances, our hearts leapt Godwards in the sheer joy of communion and oneness with Him in His will, and we gladly took our stand as the bond-slaves of Jesus Christ. It took a prison to teach Madame Guyon to sing:

> *Thy beautiful sweet will, my God,*
> *Holds fast in its sublime embrace*
> *My captive will, a gladsome bird,*
> *Prisoned in such a realm of grace.*
>
> *Within this place of certain good*
> *Love evermore expands her wings,*
> *Or nestling in Thy perfect choice,*
> *Abides content with what it brings.*

And it took our circumstances in Communist China to lead us to echo the same thoughts. The thunder-clouds that we had dreaded so much were suddenly transformed into sweet blessings. Like John Bunyan, we almost wanted to pray for greater troubles because of the greater joy they brought in God's assurances. At last our praying had ceased to be an egocentric quest for personal deliverance from trouble and had become a Theo-

centric tryst that sought first and only, "Thy will
be done on earth as it is in heaven." We ceased
trying to relate God to our problems because we
wanted to relate ourselves totally to God's
purposes, opportunities and victory.

PRAYER:

*O Father! please keep me sensitive to the
corrections of the Holy Spirit in my prayer life.
Come in like a sword-blade if You have to in
order to cut me off from my own self-seeking.
And then lead me into the joyous intimacy of
communion with Yourself in the place at Your
side for the things You are waiting to do with
me. And, O please do keep me there!*

13

"Our Father . . ."

"When ye pray say, Our Father"

It is most regrettable that what is so vital to the deep, inner meaning of prayer should have become but a traditional form in the minds of many. I am thinking particularly of what is generally called The Lord's Prayer. Seriously, how many times have you recited The Lord's Prayer without really consciously praying? Familiarity with the words and our ability to parrot them off without thinking stand in the way of our appreciating the true worth and the purpose of the content Jesus put into this prayer. If we are to find out all that was in the mind of the Savior as He taught His disciples these few words, we will need to study it carefully.

Why did Jesus teach this specific prayer and not some other? Did He give it only for those in the kindergarten stage of Christian growth and thereby conveniently exclude all those who consider themselves spiritually too mature for a prayer so elemental? I don't think so. In spite of its brevity, Jesus has put into it all the principles that we need to know as we set ourselves to learn our primary function as Christians. It is the perfect lesson by the Perfect Teacher.

The Lord Jesus, I believe, meant His prayer to be both instructive and corrective. He sets up the direction markers to start us on a one-way street. "Never will man pray as he ought," says Calvin, "unless the Master will guide both his mouth and his heart." So it is our duty to submit humbly to the pattern that is set by the Master and to correct and establish prayer habits that are not in accord with what He teaches.

Looking into the prayer, we soon see that it has two obvious divisions. The first part is clearly marked with a one-way arrow that points the thinking of the worshiper upwards to God as the worthy Object of all worship. Man's needs dominate the second part. There is a very real connection between these two worlds in this prayer. If the name of God is to be hallowed and the will of God to be done on earth, it will be through human instrumentality, because that is the way God has ordained it. So it follows that if sinful men are to perform the functions on earth that God has chosen them to fulfill, they need certain things. As men with physical bodies, they need daily bread to sustain life and give strength. Then as sinners, they need forgiveness and cleansing so that what is done for God may be acceptable. As I interpret this prayer, especially the first part, it just shouts to me, "Seek ye first the kingdom of God and His righteousness, and all these things shall be added unto you" (Matt. 6:33).

Now let us move up closer and look at just the first sentence of the Lord's Prayer—or The Learner's Prayer, for that is what it really is. Right at the start Jesus establishes a pattern of approach to God. In Matthew's Gospel the approach words are "Our Father."

While the Fatherhood of God is a concept that is mentioned in the Old Testament, it is never used as a basis of approach to God in prayer. The saintly Daniel prayed, "O Jehovah, the God of heaven, the great and dreadful God." Nehemiah prayed to the God of heaven, the great, the mighty, the terrible God. So the thought of appealing to God from the ground of an intimate relationship as children is a new mold for the disciples.

It is significant that the first word is a plural pronoun, and not the overworked "my." Because at the beginning of our prayer life the childish tendency is to be self-centered, it is the first personal pronouns *I*, *me*, and *my* that take the center of the floor. Children are born with a subjective attitude towards life's circumstances; objectivity has to be developed. As this is also true in the spiritual realm, it is one part of the Holy Spirit's work to shift the center of interest in our praying from self to God.

In considering the approach to God, I would like to suggest that there are two dimensions, the vertical and the horizontal. The word "our" infers a relationship of some sort, and I like to think that the Lord Jesus was not only thinking of our relationship in the family of God on the horizontal level down here on earth. I believe He put the

priority on our relationship with Himself and the
Holy Spirit. Surely He was trying to teach His
disciples that prayer is not just a form of words,
but worship and petition from the fact of our
relationship with Himself based on the inner
witness of the Holy Spirit of Adoption.

Our relationship with God is not inherent in us
apart from His redemptive sacrifice. He took our
nature and became the Son of Man in order that
we might receive the adoption of sons. We cannot
think of ourselves in our praying apart from Jesus
Christ, because positionally we are "in Him," and
in God's sight we are "accepted in the Beloved."
The ground of acceptance into the Father's
presence is never our right apart from or separated
from Jesus Christ. Therefore the word "our" links
us with Him and His finished work on our behalf
on the Cross. We are heard only as we abide in
Him and His words abide in us. Only then may we
ask what we will and be assured that it will be
done for us.

The words of the Lord Jesus are to influence the
whole of our conscious nature, so that whatever
flows out in prayer will harmonize with and
perfectly express His will rather than be the
outpourings of our self-centered egoism. Self, like
a Jack-in-the-box, is always trying to push aside
any restraints that are placed upon it, so that it
may burst out with its own thing. The strong
check that Jesus has given us on this is in His own
prayer to the Father, "Not My will, but Thine be
done." This vertical relationship in approaching

God is strengthened by the fact that "God hath sent forth the Spirit of His Son into your hearts crying, Abba, Father" (Gal. 4:6). Thus prayer does not spring from the isolation of my solitary *ego*, but in fellowship with the Son, who claimed, "No man cometh unto the Father but by Me." And our relationship with Him is supported by the inner witness of the Spirit of Adoption, who puts the child's cry, "Abba Father," on our lips.

It could be that the most profound reason Jesus had for selecting this pattern was to keep us from isolating ourselves from Himself and the Holy Spirit as we pray. When we say, "Our Father," the realization that we are not alone in the presence of the awesome majesty of God is immediately quickened within us. Our acceptance is complete because nothing need be added to enhance the acceptance of the Son in His Father's presence. And we need not be puzzled to know what we should pray for as we ought, because the Holy Spirit is with us to help our infirmity, not by displacing us, but by interpreting to us the mind of God as He knows it. I may be in the closet with the door shut, but the moment I open my lips to say, "Our Father," I realize that I am being drawn forward as a responsible spokesman regarding things on earth to plead as one with the Lord Jesus in His name, and with the help of the Holy Spirit.

We are probably better acquainted with the horizontal significance of the plural pronoun, "our." It reaches out to include "all saints" as we seek in prayer the will of the higher relationship at the throne for those bound up with us on the earth level in the family relationship of the Church on earth. It is in the outworking of this ministry that I find myself linking hands with God's saints in China or Cambodia, Mongolia or Mindanao, sharing in their problems and pleading for them as guided by the Holy Spirit.

These thoughts have by no means exhausted the significance of the opening words of this lesson on prayer. There is a searching quality to "Our Father" that we would sometimes like to bypass. As these words are framed with the lips, the heart attitude to some in the family can be exclusive rather than inclusive. It is easy to ignore someone that rubs us the wrong way or someone who does not think as we do on some pet issue. But there is no way that we can limit the Fatherhood of God to the ones of our choice. So there is a call, in the lesson our Lord is giving, for us to deal with our own inner hostilities and animosities. And it is completely in order that the prayer for forgiveness that follows should be qualified by our willingness to forgive those whom we tend to exclude from our praying when we pray, "Our Father,"

14

Higher Claims

"Hallowed be Thy name."

One lesson that we have to learn as we come to God is that the familiarity and security of our relationship with Him is not an invitation to us to push forward and demand what we think we need and throw tantrums until we get it. The Lord Jesus would have us preempt the claims of self for the higher claims of God's total program.

The very first petition in this prayer is, "Hallowed be Thy name." Of all the petitions that cross our lips daily, this one is hardly likely to be the first to be expressed as representing the deepest hunger in our hearts. The worldling is ready enough to call out, "O my God!" when something terrible happens. But that is only an exclamation and not a prayer. Is the Christian to follow the example of the world and call on God only when a crisis strikes? No. So this petition is put first in order to halt the impulses that drive us on our one-way street of crisis praying and to direct us to the greater need to keep the things that relate to God constantly before us.

It is the name of a person that separates him from the rest of his fellows into a category of distinctiveness that he creates for himself by his character and activity. Throughout the Bible God is very careful to point out the distinctives that are associated with His name and that separate Him from everyone else. Because God is exceedingly jealous for His name, He insists that nothing be allowed to dim its glory or cheapen its distinctives. Each time God speaks His name in Leviticus, He adds a reminder that His name is to be hallowed. It is the value of God's name that Satan is out to cheapen. Therefore to pray, "Hallowed be Thy name," is right in line with the will of God and a blow to the ambitions of Satan.

If you need help in understanding what this means, see the Lord Jesus with blazing eyes and a whip of cords in His hand driving the money-changers out of the temple. This makes a perfect picture of the attitude we ought to have toward anything in us or in our homes or across our land that dishonors God's name. We have to applaud the eight Philadelphia Councilmen who, carrying anti-pornography signs and armed with sledge-hammers, personally led an attack on the city's smut centers. If Christians were sincere in praying this prayer, it would have to have some effect on their lives and their example to the world. Jesus gives it a priority place because that is God's priority for His people.

"Thy kingdom come."

In the next petition, "Thy kingdom come," we are immediately thrown into confrontation with the kingdom of evil that opposes God's rule in the hearts of men. This petitions is the tap-root from which grows the missionary outreach of the Church. The answer that this prayer is calling for is that the Good News of salvation shall surmount every barrier Satan puts in the way and move out through the testimony of Christians to every land and people on earth. He who prays, "Thy kingdom come," has his foot pressing down hard on the accelerator of the Church's missionary outreach. This petition is from the earth and for the earth, but it does not come from human motivation. It comes from the heart of the Spirit of God, who yearns to see the power of the finished work of the Eternal Son realized to the full throughout the world.

"Thy will be done...."

Finally, "Thy will be done on earth...." In Communist China and other totalitarian states the only will that matters is the will of the Communist Party and its leaders. Any deviation in thinking from this demand for unconditional surrender of the mind is threatened with drastic punishment or death. On the other side of the scale in the shrinking free world, educators, scientists, and even our judges seem to have canceled the will of God out of their thinking in order to prop up the dignity of the individual and give him his rights to a permissive way of life that ignores completely God's absolutes. Never was the need to pray this prayer greater than it is today.

The following is adapted from *Streams in the Desert*, Vol. II, to clinch the thoughts I have expressed:

- I cannot say "OUR" unless I am aware that I am not alone in the presence of God, but united with God the Son and God the Holy Spirit.
- I cannot say "OUR" if I am shut up to the circle of my own concerns and interests, and refuse to listen to the voices of my brothers and sisters in the family of God worldwide.
- I cannot say "FATHER" apart from the Saviorhood of Jesus Christ and my acceptance in Him as God's Son, and apart from the inner witness of the Holy Spirit of Adoption.
- I cannot say "WHICH ART IN HEAVEN" without realizing that I live on earth, where the focus of rebellion to the will of God is headed up.
- I cannot say "HALLOWED BE THY NAME" unless I am prepared to take action in specific situations that dishonor the name of God in my life, my home, or in my nation.
- I cannot say "THY KINGDOM COME" unless I am ready to fight the enemies of God's kingdom and go to lands where God's kingdom still needs to come.
- I cannot say "THY WILL BE DONE" if there are any reservations in my heart concerning God's will for my life.
- I cannot say "ON EARTH AS IT IS IN HEAVEN" if I am not prepared to sacrifice anything in my heart and life that is tainted by the spirit of the world.

15

The Predictable
and the Prophesied

"Hurry! Bring your medicines and come with us!" With these words terrorists in April 1974 confronted two missionary nurses at a rural leprosy clinic in southern Thailand and took them off at gunpoint into the jungle.

The end of a defenseless lamb dragged off by a pack of ravenous wolves is so perfectly predictable that a man would have to be stupid to call in a prophet to find out the details. In nature's way of balancing things, the sheep is inherently the prey; the wolf, the predator. If we follow natural reasoning, we come up with predictable results. When we read the words of Jesus, "I send you as sheep into the midst of wolves," we tend to interpret them according to our natural reasoning. But Jesus was going beyond the natural man's way of thinking. He was looking at God's purposed end in the immediate victimizing of the sheep and at God's prophesied end when the wolves become victims of the Lamb.

God is not careless about the suffering of His sheep at the hands of the wolves. In the prey/ predator, disciple/dictator relationship there is a dimension that is shrouded in mystery. Fortunately the Bible is rich in illustrations that unshroud the mystery and help us when we are tempted to prejudge a situation.

A good illustration of the way God sends His sheep into the midst of the blood-thirsty wolfpack is found in the parable of the vineyard owner and the wicked tenant farmers. In anticipation of getting his rightful portion of the fruit, the owner sends his servants to collect. Each in turn is beaten off, stoned, or killed outright. While there is variety in the method of disposing of the servants, the purpose is one—to dispossess the owner and seize the vineyard. In spite of this, the owner's policy of sending his servants doesn't change. The predictable end of the servants and the vineyard is not considered a valid reason for changing. Having considered the expenditure of life and the apparent failure of his mission, he persists in sending. He sends, and he sends again, even to the point of calling up his last resort—the son of his heart— and commissioning him.

The explanation of this sending points back to God's sending of His servants, the prophets, and culminates in the sending of His only Son. The words of the Lord Jesus, "As the Father hath sent Me, so send I you," are His insistence to us that the sending terms have not changed, that the expenditure of suffering has been weighed and considered.

We sigh at the suffering as servant after servant goes into the arena. Human reasoning balks, chokes, and goes into gripping spasms at the ill treatment of the innocent. Why does God keep on sending when He knows perfectly well what the predictable end is going to be? Why doesn't He switch His policy, to even things up so that the prey is more fairly matched to the predator?

It is hard for us to learn that God doesn't develop a "closed-door" complex because men beat up on His sent ones and deny Him His rights. His answer to the problem will be seen at His prophesied end. There is a "hinge of history" in the unfolding drama, and when that swings, there will be a complete reversal in roles. The Lamb that was the victim will become the predator, and the wolves will become the victims.

In the parable the "hinge of history" is at the point where our Lord makes His application and is the key to the understanding of the parable. The specific time is "when . . . the Lord of the vineyard cometh." At that point of time all the earlier boasts will be exposed as premature, as will be the case in the historic context of today. The vaunted promises and predictions of world peace made by world dictators will be unveiled as premature claims, empty of any solid content.

On this side of history's hinge the predictable end is that the wolves will do away with the Lamb and His followers. On the other side, the prophe-

sied end is that wolves will be the victims of the
Lamb and His followers.

One important point needs clearing up. We do
not have to wait for the Lord of the vineyard to
come for sacrifice and suffering to be right. God is
in complete control on both sides of "the hinges."
With God the predictable and prophesied are one,
for He is the God of the eternal present tense. Yet
as we see things, on the far side of the hinge He
will punish His enemies; on this side "He maketh
the wrath of man to praise Him" (Psalm 76:10).
There is utilitarian value in the wrath of man. It is
not all rejected as unusable. The devil will never
learn the lesson. All the storm of hate that he stirs
up is used "to do whatsoever God's hand and
counsel determined before to be done." God turns
the devil's prisons into incubators for hatching out
His plans.

There is also a remnant of man's wrath that can
serve no good purpose. This God dams up and
disallows—"the remainder of wrath shalt Thou
restrain."

In God's rule there is no flaw in the prey/
predator setup. Peter tried to change it and found
himself Satan's mouthpiece. The only place
Satan's head could be bruised was at the Cross. We
have to see what Peter was made to see: God's
redemptive purposes for lost men move ahead
along a path of suffering and sacrifice. And any
diversion call is from Satan.

In God's grace we are not tied to the predicted end, for in Revelation 5 God shows through His open door at the prophesied end the "Lamb standing, as if slain," as the middle One on the throne. The Lamb merges into the Lion, the altar into the throne. John saw it in A.D. 95 so that we might believe it today.

16

Prayer —
Persuasion or
Penetration?

A familiarity with accepted prayer phraseology and an easy ability to handle it is one of the sinister vampires that all unawares has fastened onto the prayer ministry of the Church and is sucking at its vitality. The confidence we assume in prayer is that which is begotten of acquaintance with the right words. We need to examine our hearts and make sure that our confidence is forged by fellowship with the heart of the mighty Worker Himself.

We sort out our requests and then advance to the Throne to claim the answers. But somehow or other we are not too surprised when no answer is received. It all seems so hit or miss, so contrary to what the Scriptures teach. What we try to do is to persuade God to move in our direction with the answers we specify. Some problem has arisen in our little corner so we become frantic to move God to intervene on our behalf. This could be called *prayer persuasion.* It is mainly concerned with the answer sought.

If we are to approach the Throne with true confidence and begin a ministry that sees God perform wonders in answer to prayer, we must leave the *answer* for a moment and concern ourselves with the *asker.* We must know that we have God's ear, that there is nothing in us that turns His head from us or that prevents our prayer from penetrating through to His Throne of grace. This could be called *prayer penetration.* The Bible points out a number of things that roof in our praying and prevent upward penetration to God's ear.

Prayer will not penetrate Godward if I am acting presumptuously. Deuteronomy 1:45: "Ye turned and wept before the Lord; but the Lord would not hearken to your voice." It was not enough for Israel to agonize. God had told them not to go up and fight the Amorites, but they "went presumptuously." Their tears before God were inspired by the smart of punishment. The missing element was a genuine repentance toward God. Tears of self-will never persuade God to hear us. Let me search out my "presumptuous sins," and God will hear me.

Prayer will not penetrate Godward if I reject His Kingship. 1 Samuel 8:18: "Ye shall cry out in that day because of your king which ye shall have chosen . . . and the Lord will not hear you." To insist on living free from God's claims on my life will quickly block off my prayer from the Throne. The issue may be small, but to persist in a self-chosen way is fatal. Let me attend to the rebellion of my heart, and God will hear me.

Prayer will not penetrate Godward if I purposely desist from helping the needy. "Whoso stoppeth his ears at the cry of the poor, he also shall cry himself, but shall not be heard" (Proverbs 21:13). Our sensitivity is centered in things related to our own interests. Self-absorption has clogged our reception to outside calls for help. The heathen are far removed. Our lack of concern for their eternal welfare could be one valid reason for lack of prayer penetration. Let me show my real concern for God's needy, and God will hear me.

Prayer will not penetrate Godward if I regard iniquity in my heart. "If I regard iniquity in my heart, the Lord will not hear me" (Psalm 66:18). A grudge nursed against another, a sham spirituality that feeds its lean soul on the praise of men, an offended spirit that murmurs at circumstances, unwillingness to see Christ in a brother or sister, a critical spirit, trifling compromises, character flaws nursed rather than mortified will all wall up my prayers and prevent them from reaching God's audience chamber. Let me set myself to the task of cleaning house of those impurities and God will hear me.

Then and only then may I say in the confidence of faith, "Now I know that Thou hearest me," and "I know that I have the petition I desired of Him."

17

Faith — Attitude or Act?

The hymn writer who penned "What various
hindrances we meet / When coming to the mercy
seat!" could possibly have been thinking of the
two inches of snow that had just fallen or the
unexpected guests that landed on him at prayer
meeting time.

As I write I am thinking of something less
tangible but no less real. For every outward
circumstance that is allowed to keep God's children away from prayer meeting there are as many
inward things limiting the effectiveness of our
praying. Since these are less easily discerned than
the circumstantial hindrances, the Holy Spirit
must alert us to them. The outward circumstances
may hold us back from attendance at the meeting,
but it is the inward things that cause us to fall
short of God's expectations.

One of the inner ways in which we may disap-
point God is by substituting the *attitude* of faith for
the *act* of faith. Luke 8:22–25 illustrates the difference between these two concepts.

Jesus and His disciples were crossing the lake. During the passage Jesus fell asleep. Suddenly a violent storm came sweeping down over the lake, threatening their safety. The disciples hastened to rouse their Master, terrified lest all their kingdom hopes should finish up at the bottom of the lake. Rising from His slumber of exhaustion, Jesus rebuked the storm and ended the threat.

Asleep, Jesus demonstrated the *attitude* of faith. Because His trust was in God, fear had no place in His heart. This was an inner and personal attitude, altogether right and proper; but it had no effect on the predicament they were in. Awake, Jesus by an *act* of faith silenced the storm and averted the danger. Such an act was required to remove the threat from their situation and to make it possible for them to resume their course.

I believe that the purpose of the Holy Spirit in recording this dramatic incident is not just to demonstrate the mighty power of the Lord Jesus in quelling storms. The focus sharpens on the failure of the disciples, not on the success of the Master. This is borne out by the question Jesus threw at them the moment the confusion had subsided: "Where is *your* faith?" (italics mine). To me this seems to indicate His surprise at their default. Apparently they could have taken the initiative and by an act of faith saved themselves. His question implies this and expresses His concern at their cop-out.

All training is designed to equip for adequate action. Jesus was training the twelve against the day when He would no longer be physically available to them. He knew that ahead of them were storms that would threaten more than their physical safety. The assaults that He was having to face would be concentrated on them. At that time their ability to apply spiritual forces to defeat spiritual enemies would be available to them. He shared their situation and was ready whenever they might need His help. However, as their discipler, He could not but cherish the hope that their faith had progressed to the point where they would be willing to take the initiative and act.

There are still two worlds. Even as He shared the boat with His disciples, so He is with us in our troubles, undiscerned by the natural eye but nevertheless available when we cry to Him in our need. And often, when we let some trouble drive us into the corner in default of an act of faith, He asks us the same question: "Where is your faith?" He expects us to draw out our spiritual weapons and go into action as responsible, resolute men, and not to come storming hysterically into His throne room like helpless, frightened children.

When the pressure for action is on, the *attitude* of faith, justifying its hesitation to act, argues this way: "God is omniscient and sovereign. He is in control of His world and has allowed this to happen. It would be presumptuous for us to do more than just put our trust in Him and let Him work out the circumstances in His way and in His time."

But it is not God's will as Supreme Ruler to overthrow and sweep away all the forces of evil by the might of His omnipotent arm. His government is so ordered that prayer is one of its vital constituent parts. In the work of creation God needed no help. He worked sovereignly and alone. One breath of His commanding word, and the stars of heaven were formed and marshaled into their appointed places.

However, in His redemptive activity through history God does not work alone. He no longer remains aloof in His heaven. Man the sinner can only be redeemed by Man the Savior. God must partake of flesh and blood, dealing with man through men. Even as He sent the eternal Son to be incarnated as "God with us," so He has ordained that redeemed men shall embody His will on earth.

The continuing struggle for the triumph of God's beneficent will over the demonic will of destructive spirits is not carried out with men sitting it out as spectators on the sidelines. Our part in the conflict is carried out in the effort of prayer—and I mean effort—as we strive to know His will, to side with it and to embody it. It is this process that unlocks the door of God's self-imposed limitation and frees Him to move out into the situation and execute His will. To use Dr. Moberly's words, "He bids His own work wait on man's prayers."

Our spiritual fathers were surefooted and at home in the activity of faith. One senses, however, that these words would not fairly describe the attitude of our own generation. It is our practice that gives us away, not our profession. We are apologetic, not dynamic, tending to play down the value of spiritual faith that acts. We still believe in prayer and the attitude of faith. We do not hesitate to tell God all about our particular difficulty. We describe it for Him, explain how it all happened and what it is doing to hinder His work. Then, just so that we do not exceed our prerogatives in asking Him to intervene, we attach our appendage formula, "If it be Thy will," and send our prayer on its way.

In Mark 11:23 Jesus lays down His formula for dealing with obstacles. He specifies a case in which the attitude of faith must extend itself into an act of faith. "Say unto this mountain," He says, "Be thou removed, and be thou cast into the sea." We busy ourselves praying about the mountains. Jesus tells us that there are times when faith must be expressed in directives issued to mountains.

Many mountains obstruct the progress of God's work in the world today. They are there by default, and the blame is on us. As long as the mountains persist, we will never be able to see what God has for us on the other side. It would be a timely exercise for us to revise our estimates on the value of faith as a spiritual force in the work and warfare of God. Our calling and function is not to replace God, but to release Him. Nor do we have to overcome any reluctance on His part. It has been rightly said, "Without God man cannot; without man God will not."

"The ministry of the church," said the late Watchman Nee, "includes the bringing down to earth of the will that is in heaven." This is to be done by diligent application in prayer, through the power of God the Holy Spirit and in the name of God the Son, pressing importunately for the victorious goal of all true prayer, "Thy will be done in earth, as it is in heaven."

18

Authority —
Assumed or Authentic?

Picture, if you will, seven hippies on the run. Streaking after them with murder in his eyes is a screaming maniac. Escape they cannot. The madman tears into them, leaving them badly mauled and well-chastened.

In case you haven't recognized the contemporary version of Acts 19:13–17, this is the story of "seven sons of one Sceva, a chief of the priests." I call them hippies because I know of no better contemporary word to describe them. Obviously they are disenchanted with the "establishment" and, associating with a bunch of vagabond Jews, have taken to a vagrant form of life. They have rejected alike the comfortable style of living in the home of a chief of the priests, and the dead formalism which that home symbolized. The "in" thing of this particular group was dabbling in the occult. Because Paul had notable success in calling the name of Jesus over demon-possessed men, they thought to try the same technique. Tragically for them, the demon challenged their authority to intrude into this particular field, and the results we have already seen. Theirs was demonstrated to be an *assumed authority*.

Authority is a touchy subject, but chiefly because it is one of the symbols of the establishment in today's thinking. We cannot think of one without thinking of the other. But the real significance of authority is seen beyond the outward symbols. It is the right of power to act in a given situation. The surgeon at the operating table with the scalpel in his hand has authority to operate— not because he has the instrument in his hand, but because behind him stands his school with all its wealth of knowledge and tested experience. Having submitted him to its disciplines and training, the school attests his right to operate.

The seven sons of Sceva tried to steal an authority that was not theirs by adding the postscript "in Jesus' name." Their discomfiture by the demon should be a warning to us. In the inevitable clash with the powers of evil arrayed to overthrow the work of God, no assumed authority will avail. Going through the motions is not good enough. Words alone, no matter how religious, have no intrinsic power. On such occasions, prayer is a clash of rival authorities, and the enemy will only yield to the authority that is personally related to Jesus Christ. The implication from this story for us today is that demon powers should be able to say, "Jesus I know, and John Smith I know." The question is, do the demons have my name on the list of those with delegated authentic right to command?

Over against this demonstration of assumed authority from Acts 19, there is a lesson on *authentic authority* in Exodus 17.

To supply the critical shortage in Israel's camp of the desert's most precious commodity, God commands Moses to take his rod and smite the rock. Moses strikes the rock, and the life-giving water starts flowing. Just as the people are enjoying this miraculous provision for their need, a sneak attack is made by a band of desert marauders, jealous of Israel's privileges and wanting the water for themselves.

What does Moses do in this crisis? If Moses is going to give us an example of the kind of praying God responds to in this sort of a crisis, we will need to watch him closely. Does he fall on his face and call on God for deliverance as he did at the Red Sea when Pharaoh's chariots threatened? This is what we would expect him to do, and I think that this is what we would do in similar circumstances. Does he run to his tent, or to the tent of meeting to pray and ask Joshua to send him prayer bulletins by express carrier so that he can pray intelligently regarding the progress of the conflict with Amalek? No, he does neither of these two things. Instead he turns away from the camp, and under the astonished gaze of the people, deliberately and purposefully makes his way to the hill-top that dominates the scene of the fighting.

It may seem strange to us that Moses should leave the area where he was most needed, but there was very good reason for his action. He was separating himself from the local situation in order to gain altitude and resist the real enemy that was attacking the people of God. God could have heard him just as easily had he cried from the bottom of the sea, or from the floor of his tent; so obviously Moses is not trying to get closer to God's ear. There is praying that looks up to God from a position of stress or danger, a cry from the depths, the appeal of an overwhelmed soul. There is also an exercise that is demonstrated in this passage in which the servant of God initiates a confrontation with the enemy in his high places with the rod of God in his hand, the symbol of delegated authority.

This is what Paul is writing about in Ephesians 6:10ff. Moses on the mountain represents the position of the believer in the heavenly places in Christ, far above all principalities and powers. The stretched out rod represents authentic delegated authority. The war was not with the Amalekites first, but with the supernatural powers of darkness in the heavenlies. Such wrestling does not fit the category of "a wee spot of prayer," and Moses found out how tiring it could be.

God's instruction for Moses and for us, in this exercise of delegated authority, began when,

pointing to the rod Moses was carrying as a
shepherd, He asked him, "What is that in thine
hand?" This was preliminary to the commissioning of Moses for the task of leading Israel out from
under the bondage of Pharaoh. God was teaching
him that the man He sends goes as His ambassador
with His authority, and God used the rod as the
symbol of the authority that was his as God's
commissioned servant.

At Rephidim, for the first time, Moses does not
wait for God to command him to stretch out the
rod against the enemy in the heavenlies. And this
is the only time Moses initiates action with the rod
without special instructions from God. God's
honor is involved. His blessings for His people are
being stolen, and His people are under attack.
Therefore the powers of evil that are responsible
for this must be challenged. His outstretched
hands on the hilltop are not stretched out in
entreaty but in authority. He owns the rod that
God owns and honors. He knows that the wicked
spirits must say, "God we know, and Moses we
know." His right to act and the power of his
authority are proved authentic on the ground by
the victory that Joshua wins as the hands with the
rod are stretched out.

The question now is, how can we take this
lesson and make it our own? Let us look at it
propositionally:

Local attacks are visible evidence of a declara-

tion of war by the invisible, but very real enemy, "the prince of the power of the air."

- Are local authorities taking action to keep the Gospel messengers from doing their job?
- Are Bibles being denied right of entry to some people or tribe?

If so, then we may be sure that there is a storm of fury above the local situation. The storm on the lake that threatened the lives of Jesus and His disciples was the indication of a higher hate, and it was to that higher hate that Jesus spoke his rebuke to still the waves.

For every provocation against God's cause there is provision for victory.

Victory is an accomplished fact, but it does need a man to lay hold of that victory and precipitate a confrontation with the enemy, and resist him. The Scripture tells us to "Watch unto prayer," that is, to watch and be alert to the assaults of the enemy in order to withstand him.

19

My Praying, or My Prayer

The Apostle Paul is a great teacher on prayer. Not that he wittingly sets out to develop techniques on how to pray. His teaching comes to us from his example, not from precepts laid down. And what a vital, vibrant thing his prayer life was! One minute joy bubbles and overflows, as exciting news comes from one of the churches he had "wrought with labor and travail night and day" to bring to the birth. In the next, spiritual muscles are straining. The battle is on, and we become aware of a reality and intensity that seems exaggerated to those who have only attended twentieth-century church prayer meetings. With undisguised honesty he spreads the burdens and joys before the Lord. This in itself is a lesson.

We would be inclined to shrink (I would) from the public exposure of our inner prayer life. That could be because there is so little room for God's longings in the cluttered prayer chamber of our hearts. We are not in the habit of visiting this hallowed place often enough, nor do we stay long

enough to generate any fervor. The casualness of
our attitude towards this most important part of
Christian living, together with the shallowness of
our desires, are enough reason to avoid the exposure of our prayer life. Fenelon's comment, "He
who desires not from the depth of his heart makes
a deceitful pray-er," fits our case too often.
However, spiritual deceits are self-retaliatory and
will teach us as no lesson book can that "God
desires truth in the inward parts."

But Paul is not afraid to disclose what is in his
heart, because its contents are the love and longing of God's heart that he has adopted as his own,
and for which he has surrendered his personal
desires. Significant prayer activity is not self-
stimulated. Paul's wrestling and watchings may
have taken place in lonely night vigils, but they
were not undertaken alone. The pressure that
brought on the prayer started at a higher level. His
life was "hid with Christ in God." To Paul, being
seated with Christ in heavenly places meant that
he shared the perspective of the Church's Head.
Faith's appropriation of this living union with the
mighty Conqueror caused the throb in the deeps
of God's heart to pulse through Paul's heart.
Divine and human desire glowed and merged
together in response to the call of specific need.

It was this sort of a situation that was seen in
Sialkot, North India, prior to the revival. "Three
renewed human wills that by faith linked themselves as with hooks of steel to the omnipotent
will of God ... yearning, pleading, crying and

agonizing over the church in India and the myriads of lost souls." For twenty-one days and nights Hyde, Paterson and Turner, the three leaders of the Punjab Prayer Union, were totally absorbed in praying, believing and praising for the outpouring of God's blessing and power on the convention delegates. Certainly efforts of such intensity and depth can only be understood in terms of the communion of compulsiveness as man willingly becomes the channel for the yearning of God's heart.

And so as Paul reads in Isaiah of God's longings over Israel, God's heartache preempts all other claims and takes over his heart. He sees the pathos of a situation where God is left stretching out His hands all day long in pleading entreaty to a disobedient and obstinate people. This becomes so much a part of him that he bursts out, "Brethren, my heart's desire and [*my*] *prayer* to God for Israel is, that they might be saved." The heaven-born desire of his heart had fanned into flame his prayer, and the prayer exposed the intensity and longing of his heart.

However, when Paul is talking about "*my prayer*," I think he means more than *my praying*. Rightly or wrongly, we equate these two concepts; yet there can be a very real difference between them. *My praying* is my attempt to clothe heart content with suitable words, words that will conform to the forms set by the groups in which I do my praying. It is praying within the bounds set

by certain cultural patterns. Moreover, it is suscep-
tible to physical conditions—the hour, the nature
of the occasion, and the audience. In *my praying* I
find it hard not to be self-conscious and crowd-
conscious. These factors do intrude and, depend-
ing on my temperament, dilute the flow of the
inner spiritual longing.

"*My prayer*," on the other hand, is heart content,
separate from word content. It is neither bound by
word forms nor inhibited by the listening
audience. It is the overflow of a heart that the
Holy Spirit has rendered sensitive to spiritual
issues in earthly situations, poured out in a steady,
uninhibited stream of undiluted longing.

"*My prayer*" is not identified apart from me. I
give it the identity Heaven seeks. Gabriel comes to
Zacharias to tell him, "Zacharias, thy prayer is
heard. . . ." Though the couple may have stopped
praying for a son, the identity of the prayer in
Heaven is linked with a man on earth.

I conceive of "*my prayer*" as that spiritual
purpose God has laid on my willing, yielded
heart, sometimes voiced back to Him and sometimes just choked in unutterable groanings. It is as
though God is saying to me, "Take this child and
nurse it for me." At His instigation I take, adopt as
my own, and assume foster-parent responsibilities
for nurturing this specific purpose of God to its
planned maturity. And this is to be done, not in
my own willing and strength, but by the inner
constraint of God's Holy Spirit in my spirit, press-

ing me to this duty of adoption and enabling me
for its every involvement.

"*My prayer*" is the end of the Divine search for a
man to stand in the gap and to intercede for a
people doomed to destruction by their own sin
and headstrong rejection of God's authority in
their natural life. Abraham "stood yet before the
Lord" when the Lord was on His way to execute a
sentence of doom on Sodom and Gomorrah for
their sin. Moses stood in the breach before God to
turn away His wrath from destroying Israel. And
Paul, with the same spirit of self-sacrifice, sighs, "I
could wish that I myself were anathema from
Christ for my brethren's sake." These men were
willing to sheath the flaming blade of God's judgment in their own hearts, and in this they were
not alone—there was Another:

> *Jehovah bade His sword awake,*
> *O Christ, it woke 'gainst Thee!*
> *Thy blood the flaming blade must slake;*
> *Thy heart its sheath must be.*

Mrs. Cousins

He stood in the gap to "bear the sin of many and
make intercession for the transgressors."

"*My prayer*" is the cry that comes from earth's
lonely desert places "a great while before day." It
is hands lifted desperately to midnight skies—

> *How have I knelt with arms of my aspiring*
> *Lifted all night in irresponsive air,*
> *Dazed and amazed with overmuch desiring,*
> *Blank with the utter agony of prayer.*

F. W. H. Meyers

The sleeping pill is the enemy of this kind of praying. Uninvolved Christianity has little inclination for the sacrifice of time and convenience demanded. Consequently the church, like the "ram caught by his horns," has lost its attack power—and this at a time when the devil is deploying his forces for a grand assault. But for those willing to commit themselves to Christ for this kind of warfare, enlistment could well be the watershed of their lives. On one side half-developed values, wrong priorities, and a frustrated casting around for spiritual shortcuts to exorcise a sense of failure. But over the watershed new standards are discovered and new touchstones. We learn how few things are really essential and how essential those few things really are. One of these is *"my prayer."*

> *But here it dwells, and here must I*
> *With danger seek it forth;*
> *To spend the time luxuriously*
> *Becomes not men of worth.*

> **Daniel**

20

Perspective

**"He makes the (storm) clouds His chariot"
(Psalm 104:3).**

Through the mouth of His prophet-evangelist
Isaiah, God declares, "For as the heavens are
higher than the earth, so are My ways than your
ways, and My thoughts than your thoughts." Our
human perspective on current events is naturally
low-centered. We tend to look at the circumstances of life in terms of what they may do to our
cherished hopes and convenience, and we shape
our decisions and reactions accordingly. When a
problem threatens, we rush to God, not to seek His
perspective, but to ask Him to deflect the trouble.
Our self-concern takes priority over whatever it is
that God might be trying to do through the trouble. One of the harder lessons of life is to learn
that our low-centered, sense-oriented subjectivism
militates against our effective cooperation with
God in His purpose for us in a given trial.

In order to bring this point home to us, I want to
introduce you to Daniel, a Daniel you may not be

too well acquainted with. The teenage part of his life is generally skipped over because of the interesting things that happened later. Watch with this fourteen-year-old as the trumpet blast alerts Jerusalem to the approach of Nebuchadnezzar's army, sending shivers down the boy's spine and setting the whole city agog with fear and confusion. Feel with him as cruel hands separate him from loved ones and herd him into the group destined for captivity. Walk with him in the captive train as he is driven from his beloved country across the weary, dusty miles to Babylon. With each step hope sinks lower, and physical discomforts sap his spiritual stamina. And then pray with him as he anticipates the ruthless pressures of monopolized life in a totalitarian state, without the accustomed religious props.

But how do you pray in a situation like this? What are you to pray for? What chance will there be of being any use to God or country as a captive in a heathen country? How do you pray when your storehouse of hope and promise is suddenly emptied, and the future turns into a dead-end street? How are you to confront God with the fact that your life potential and possible usefulness to Him has just been canceled out?

Thousands of others besides Daniel have had to face similar situations. For them and for us Daniel has some strong meat. It is the sort of circumstance that Daniel had to face that matures us and drives us to seek God, not just for our relief, but for His own sake. Let us turn to Daniel's book to see what the young captive has to say about this terrible situation that has befallen him and his people and about the mission of God in the world.

In verse one he gives us the low-centered human perspective on the news—"In the third year of Jehoiakim king of Judah came Nebuchadnezzar king of Babylon unto Jerusalem and besieged it." He is no doubt quoting the scribe-chronicler, the equivalent to our TV newscaster, as he gives the bare who, what, when, and where of the event. From the human perspective all we can see is the initiative of a man. Man is in the center of the stage and God nowhere in the circumference because, as far as the news media are concerned, God is not a relevant factor in what happens. The man behind the mike sees only the results. What he does not see are the intangible, yet real determinative principles, which, because they are based on God's unchanging absolutes, are the direct cause of the results he is reporting.

In the second verse Daniel soars to give us the divine perspective—"The Lord gave Jehoiakim . . . into his [Nebuchadnezzar's] hand." While the news reporter sees only the Nebuchadnezzars, the Herods, and the Maos beating up a storm, Daniel from a higher perspective see these same storm clouds as the chariots of the Lord's redemptive conquest. He insists that political changes are controlled and used by God for His own purposes. On this particular trip the Lord's chariot—Nebuchadnezzar's invasion army—has two goals to accomplish. Though one relates to Babylon and one to Israel, both will be taken care of at the same time.

First, God will have His truth witnessed to in Babylon; so there is a planting work for Nebuchadnezzar to do. The motivation of God in this world's affairs is redemptive. He will have all men to be saved and come to a knowledge of the truth, but He does need and has chosen to use men to be His instruments as witnesses and intercessors. Babylon is on God's heart just as Nineveh was when He sent Jonah to preach there. But where is He to get a man? In a spirit of unrelenting isolationism, the people of Israel have detached themselves from any responsibility toward the nations surrounding them.

So, then, God's goal for Israel is two-fold: to punish her flagrant sins and also to correct this isolationism. It is at this point in history (Dan. 1:2) that God deliberately turns over the sovereignty of the nations to heathen kings—under His supreme control, of course—for a predetermined duration and for a designed end. The tragedy in Judah and the evacuation of the Shekinah from the temple in Jerusalem, a city "set in the midst of the nations," is not an indication that God is throwing in the sponge and abdicating His control—far from it! It is just that God is changing His work pattern. The light that was at the center is now to be scattered out into the darkness, and God has His eye on Daniel, Hananiah, Mishael, and Azariah to be the spearhead for His new missionary approach. His selected team of faithful, fearless witnesses will be taken to their mission field at Nebuchadnezzar's expense, by his army. And at the same time the decreed punishment will fall on Israel. God here uses the same instrument to do the punishing and the planting.

We revert to our earlier question. How do you pray when the future suddenly becomes a dead-end street? Daniel has taught us that above the dead-end streets of human perspective there is the divine perspective that unfolds limitless opportunities within the will of God. God fulfills Himself in many ways. Jonah's witness might be given on the street corners of Nineveh, but Daniel's band had to give theirs in the fire and in the lions' den. In both places the results were dramatic and effective. Nowhere is the greatness of God seen to such advantage as it is in His ability to use as His chariot of conquest the circumstances that pose the greatest threat to His cause.

21

Opportunity Price Tag

Most missionary societies publish an annual list of service opportunities. But opportunity is not just a collection of assorted goodies set before us to drool over while we try to decide which one we really want. Avowedly, young people want to serve the Lord, to know His will. Yet when it comes to making a selection for summer, short-term, or long-term service, personal preference rather than principle often influences the choice. Perhaps the main reason is that they are unaware of the principles involved in opportunity selection.

As a commodity in God's market, opportunity is spiritual in content, even though it has very practical and personal implications. The danger comes when we allow the spiritual content to be submerged under practical considerations. As a market commodity, it comes with a price tag. In the States or Canada or anywhere in the free world it might take a bit of time and effort, or courage (not very much) to buy up God's opportunity. But in China, Cuba, or Russia, where the price is subject to wild inflation, it could cost all that a man has to take a stand for his faith and to bear witness to Jesus Christ. And let's not kid ourselves that the price will decline if we stay out of the market. In these inflationary times, all indications point to a rising cost in the price of opportunity. Detente is but the expression of our wishful, but unrealistic thinking. It is the sinuous silk glove that masks the iron hand.

God's redemptive opportunities never come disguised. Jesus Christ doesn't coerce men to follow Him by pandering to the tastes of the natural man. He doesn't sugar-coat His opportunities and then dangle them in front of us to lure us on. All opportunities on His list have a fixed price—*sacrifice*. They are available to those who repudiate self's claims.

A prospective missionary once came to me with this question: "Would it be possible for you to arrange for me to be sent where the communists won't come?" He was wanting to fit the opportunity for preaching the Gospel into the limited perspective of the circumference of his personal security. If we could arrange this for him, he would be in the market, otherwise not at all. He had to learn that God's price is fixed and how bankrupt he was of the currency God asks in exchange for His opportunity.

Teenager Daniel and his three friends, trudging wearily across the desolate wastes toward Babylon as Nebuchadnezzar's captives, could have argued that all opportunity for serving God was over as far as they were concerned. And who would have blamed them? Deported out of the land of their fathers by a cruel tyrant, torn from comfortable homes and separated from loved ones, surely they were facing the end of opportunity. Nothing could have looked less like an open door for life service than captivity in Babylon.

Today Christians in China or Russia face a comparable situation in the accusations, arrests, and deportations to Tibet or Siberia that they endure for Christ's sake. They, too, could plead that the door is closed and their opportunity to serve the Lord over. No doubt many have looked at the price tag even as they did in Daniel's day and have lost interest in involvement for God.

It is time we sought God's definition of a closed door and forget some of our own. When we hear the wolves howling, we think we have to rush for cover, lest we get hurt. Jesus saw things the other way. He said to His disciples, "I send you as sheep into the midst of wolves." We are not justified in arguing that a door is closed just because danger is threatening. Paul's reasoning endorses the Savior's remarks. He says, "Buy up the opportunity, *because* the days are evil." It was this that gave Watchman Nee his text when he returned to Shanghai under the communists in 1949 and found many of his friends preparing to escape. He himself was outside China at the time of Mao's takeover and could have stayed in the free world if he had heeded the advice of his friends. But in prayer God had showed him that his responsibilities lay in China. Daniel was taken captive to his assignment—he had no choice as to place. Watchman Nee was captive in another sense as he declared his intention of going back into the lions' den.

We have noted that the captivity of Israel in Babylon had two sides. God's judgment on Israel's sin does not so dominate His thoughts that all other concerns are forgotten. Love precedes wrath, and the saving of man takes precedence over the punishing of man. God is redemptive before He is punitive. His Lamb submits meekly to being sacrificed on the altar before He rides forth to judge and make war. God's love sent Jonah to Nineveh and placed Daniel in Babylon with His punishment of Israel. What we see as a closed door in Babylon was closed only to those who rejected the price tag on God's opportunity. The door in China is closed only to those who are not willing to pay the price of making an opportunity.

Daniel and his three friends were placed where God wanted them, but it was up to them to make the opportunity for God. By purposing in their hearts not to yield one iota in their God-inspired convictions, they burst open the door of opportunity in a closed land. The faithful captives brought the tyrant dictator to his face before them, confessing, "Blessed be the God of Shadrach, Meshach, and Abednego, who hath sent His angel, and delivered His servants that trusted in Him...."

The price tag on this opportunity was, Don't bow, but burn—don't give in; get thrown in. They bought it.

The prisons and labor camps of China's bitter northwest are mute testimony to a similar faithful witness that has refused to be silenced by Mao and his party. No door is closed where men and women are prepared to cling to their convictions and refuse to be conformed to the squeeze of the world.

22

The Architect of Victory

> There is a divine principle in regard to prayer which runs all through the Scriptures. It is that God is pleased to unite His people with Himself in whatever He is about to do. He first of all leads them to pray, and then does what He intends in answer to their prayers.
>
> **Russell Elliott**

When the Bible records an incident that is directly the occasion of special prayer and God's subsequent answer to that prayer, that incident and all that leads up to it has to be most important. To give it less than the closest study is to miss the privilege of learning God's ways. The work of God's people is to pray, but under normal conditions we are reluctant to take time out of the stream of "religious" activity that rushes us along imprisoned between its banks. However, let misfortune or catastrophe strike us or ours, and then, in proportion to the desperateness of the trouble, we will pray. But the work of God requires a maturer and less self-centered approach, and this is where God comes into the picture.

All prayer first begins with God before it is taken up on earth. His will is the only focus of all true prayer. He has been over all the circumstances that make up the situation and knows what needs to be done. But He restrains action until a call reflecting His will comes from earth. Only the prayer that finds its expression through a will that is captive to His desiring can be assured of a hearing at the Throne of Grace. To achieve this, God sometimes arranges a set of circumstances that will lay a burden of constraint on someone to direct specific prayer toward the particular thing He is wanting to accomplish. The Spirit-sensitized soul seeking after God's will in the circumstances becomes aware of what God is aiming to do, so gives himself to prayer to seek its accomplishment.

This process of God at work, engineering circumstances to provoke a prayer that will give Him the opportunity to involve Himself in the situation, is very clearly shown in the story of Nebuchadnezzar's dream (Daniel 2). Side-tracked into studying only the dream's prophetic significance, we can all too easily miss the central and important thing I think the Holy Spirit is trying to teach: that prayer must be made in order that God may move into the situation to work out His purposed dispositions. It is this fact that links together all the threads of this chapter. Each part finds its explanation in the leading of God to bring about a particular prayer in order to produce certain results in the kingdom of this heathen dictator.

Now come to the story. The glory of Judah and
Jerusalem has suffered a total eclipse. Black night
has settled over the land. The army of Nebuchadnezzar first express their contempt of Jehovah by
taking some of the vessels from the temple to
place before the gods of Babylon. And then the
choicest of the people and the king's seed are
taken captive.

Among those driven or dragged to this center of
evil was Daniel. As a teenager he could easily have
resented what life was dishing up to him, letting it
embitter him for the rest of his life. Indeed, who
would blame Daniel for thinking that everything
was hopelessly lost? But because Daniel had been
brought up in the school of the Scriptures and
under Jeremiah, his perspective was not limited to
human factors. He seemed to realize that his
appointed place of witness was to be right at the
power-center of Satan's rebellion capital of the
world. His new home town was to be Babylon, the
devil's brewery where the heady wine of hostility
to God was fermented.

In the matter of how and where he was to serve
the Lord, Daniel was given no choice, but like
Joseph was taken to his place of service by cruel
men, motivated by pride and envy. God has more
than one way of getting His servants to the place
where He wants them to serve. He is the Architect
of every beneficent purpose of redemptive grace.
He selects the best circumstances from His
perspective in which His chosen ones will have
the opportunity to give their witness for Him. His

selection supersedes the purposing of the mightiest of earth's despots.

Because from our limited human viewpoint we sometimes cannot see that our place of appointment makes sense, we struggle against it. In the apparent mistakes of life, the way to peace is not found in struggling against circumstances nor by trying to escape, but in accepting all that comes as the "good and acceptable and perfect will of God," chosen by an all-wise God as best suited for attaining His goals.

In the interplay between the redemptive purposes of God and the destructive opposition of the evil powers seen in chapter two of Daniel, there are five distinct parts, two pairs and one central pivot:

A Dictator's Dream   *The Desire of Daniel*   *The Divine Disclosure*
A Dictator's Decree   *The Divine Dispositions*

The muscle that ties this skeleton outline of the chapter is the meeting of the prayer cell.

I. A Dictator's Dream

In order to understand the real significance of the fact that the king dreamed, we must go beyond natural causes and seek out the divine reason. I mean that the dream was not a nightmare brought about by wild feasting. The explanation is given later by Daniel, when he tells the king, "The great God hath made known to the king. . . ." As Nebuchadnezzar lay sleeping, God flashed a dream-picture on the screen of his subconscious mind. The grand slam at the end of the dream, when the stone hit the image and shattered it to smithereens, frightened the king out of his slumber. Startled awake, he is aware that a higher power is threatening his visions of the development and future glory of Babylon as the continuing world power. In his desperation he wakens the palace and gives orders for all the wise men, astrologers, and magicians to appear before him.

Whatever lay behind the secrets of the invisible world and whatever would help disclose those secrets was sought after as precious treasure and held in high esteem by the Babylonians. Since the days of Nimrod and the Tower of Babel, Babylon was the place where men delved into the occult and hidden mysteries. This was their strong point, and it is at this point that God is going to show them their weakness and His superiority. God alone knows the future. As the devil's knowledge of the future is limited to what God has been pleased to reveal, there is no way that he can help his team of magicians find answers to the king's problems. But for some reason the king seems determined to expose the wise men for a bunch of fakes. He demands that they not only tell him the explanation of the dream, but first describe what it was that he dreamed about. God is stripping Satan of his armor.

In this dramatic play of events God is creating a set of circumstances that will lead to a prayer, which in turn will bring Him into the situation to change it to forward His own purposes of grace. Notice that God starts with Satan's number-one man. In doing this God is illustrating a principle. He deals with peoples through their authority figures, and that is why we are told to pray for "kings and all in authority" (1 Timothy 2:2).

In this situation God needs His man close to the king. In order to get him there, God chooses to give the king a dream. But the jealous wise men of Babylon are not going to let Daniel steal their thunder; so he is left at home while they hurry off to the palace.

But in taking the initiative in this way, God has softened the king's defenses. The world ruler is suddenly obsessed with fears, feeling very insecure in the frightening awareness of a power threat that he has no resources to cope with. He certainly does not seem to trust his wise men. Obviously God alone knows the answers. God has shut up the whole situation to prayer. Even Daniel has no way of knowing the king's dream without God's help.

II. A Dictator's Decree

The king orders the destruction of all the wise men unless they are able to tell him his dream. The only one able to bring a change to this fearful situation is God. This the sorcerers willingly acknowledge as they stall for time and the opportunity to arrange for a compromise, and this the king is not about to grant. Satan is not out to get his men executed, but he is willing to sacrifice

them if by doing so he can exterminate Daniel and
his three friends. Remember, he was a murderer
from the beginning. He figures that God has over-
stepped Himself and played into his hands by
causing the king to dream, and now there is
nothing to stop him from scuttling the purposes of
God in one fell swoop.

But Satan's vision is limited. Little does he
realize that his brilliantly conceived master-stroke
is to bring about the very thing he fears most and
against which he has no power to prevail. The
decree of Nebuchadnezzar is going to drive
Daniel to his knees to seek the answer from the
One he knows will alone be able to fit the key and
unlock the mystery. On earth God's last toehold
may appear to be disintegrating with the dilemma
that threatens His helpless remnant. But in actual
fact, He knows all about the decree of the king,
and rather than restrain it, He is going to use it.
This, more than anything else, will give the right
direction to the prayers of His faithful friends. If
the decree does succeed in getting Daniel to pray,
then Satan will have supplied God with the
instrument He seeks in order to give the cruel
enemy his *coup de grace*. Everything hinges on
what happens next. The issues lie with a man and
his prayer. So watch and see how Daniel acts in
this crisis.

III. The Desire of Daniel
There is very grave danger in confronting a
frustrated despot, but in Daniel's mind this is

completely offset by the urgency of the situation
and the fact of God. I am sure he is aware that it is
God who has spoken to the king in the dream and
that He has a specific purpose for doing this.
Therefore if he should be killed off at this point,
all that God is intending to do will revert to
"square one." As the secret that is involving so
many lives is tied up with God, the key on earth
lies with the man who is in touch with God. Not
only do the lives of many depend on that man, the
whole purpose of God is locked into him. It is this
thought that stiffens the backbone in Daniel that
had refused to bend in an earlier test of his loyalty
to God.

Another factor emboldens Daniel as he contem-
plates the need for someone to confront the king.
It is the assurance that God does hear and will
respond to the prayers of His children in their
times of need. He realizes that prayer is the master
key to defuse the destructive decree. However,
time is of the essence. So hurrying to the palace,
he "desired of the king that he would give him
time." The assurance of Daniel's faith must have
communicated itself to the king, for without hesitation the king grants the request, though he had
denied the same request to the wise men earlier.

I would like to have walked home with Daniel
as he left the palace in order to ask him about the
things that were going through his mind. Did he
read the situation as a mere threat to life? Or, did
he perceive that the physical danger was but the
tip of the iceberg and an evidence that there were

implications not discernible to the natural senses?
I think by this time he had come to realize that the
crux of the whole matter was bound up in his
being able to stay alive. How else could God's
message be conveyed to the king? It was not that
he feared the uncomfortable and messy business
of being beheaded, but because "dead men tell no
tales," and he is sure that God wants him to give
the king a message.

Reaching home, he knows what must be done if
the situation is to be saved, and save it he must. He
gathers his faithful prayer cell around him, and
together they "desire mercies of the God of heaven."

Many of God's afflicted servants have planted
their faith on the psalmist's word, "I shall not die,
but live, and declare the works of the Lord" (Ps.
118:17). Living is not to be the end sought, but the
means to God's end. The works of the Lord must
be declared. The king must be made to realize that
the message of the dream is from the one and only
true and living God of all the earth and heaven,
and not from any lower source that the magicians
and sorcerers might have recourse to. Furthermore
Daniel must be credited in the king's eyes as being
God's representative and qualified to speak with
authority on His behalf to king or commoner.
Everything hinges on prayer. There is no alterna-
tive solution, and there will be no turning point of
salvation apart from prayer. Having maneuvered
to get His team on their knees, pleading according
to His will, God is now free to join the action, for

this is just what He has purposed that prayer should do.

IV. The Divine Disclosure

The lesson here is this: God will not do apart from prayer what He can do through prayer. This unusual drama was set in motion as God made the first move. But notice that following the dream, all the activity is on the earth plane until the prayer meeting in Daniel's home. After causing the king to dream, God has maintained a waiting posture until the prayers of the little band free Him from His self-imposed limitations. Responding immediately, God reveals the dream and its interpretation to Daniel. Back to the palace goes Daniel. Not to steal the glory for himself. Carefully and deliberately he draws the attention of the king to the greatness of God. Then he sees to it that the wise men and sorcerers are duly discredited before he gets down to the business of recalling to the king his dream and then giving the interpretation. What a climax!

V. The Divine Dispositions

In the last four verses of the chapter we have the list of things God was planning when He opened the act:

- Nebuchadnezzar the king is doing homage to one of his captives.
- Satan's king is giving testimony publicly to the fact that God is indeed the God of gods and Lord of kings.

- God's man is appointed ruler of the province of Babylon.
- The others in God's team are given government appointments.
- Some bad men are displaced, and the tricksters are discredited.

The political structure of Satan's rebellion-capital is changed by God's working to create a crisis at the top and leading His men at the bottom to pray. We ought to ask ourselves, Is there a country in the world today that does not have a crisis at the top? Are God's people among the rank and file showing sensitivity towards God's attempts to unite them with Himself in what He wants to do through the world's authority figures? He needs us to plead for kings and those in authority (1 Timothy 2:1–4). For the world to hear God's message, Christians must believe with Daniel that the purpose in living is to secure through prayer the opportunity to proclaim God's sure word of prophecy.

In all of this, what has God accomplished? He has given Daniel a new understanding of his God and of His own controlling role in world history. He has changed a dictator's theology. And He has rearranged the government of Babylon by displacing four bad men and replacing them with His own good men. Then, as far as we are concerned, He has taught us the place and purpose of prayer in the conflict with evil powers that oppose His will.

23

Faith's Alternates

There will always be times in life when the expectations of our faith will not be realized in the way we anticipated. For example, a young person fired with zeal to serve God applies for service overseas and is turned down by the mission board. Or a young couple, in love and convinced that the Lord wants them together, happily plan for their marriage. A war comes along, knocking the bottom out of their starry world. (The writer speaks from experience on both counts.) Situations such as these and a hundred and one others quickly show how faith's confident expectations can be ruthlessly contradicted and fail to reach fruition at the time and in the way we thought. But the very fact that God does at times sovereignly intervene to upset our best-laid schemes ought to encourage us. He only purposes to refine our planning and to eliminate any unworthy, self-centered determination that may have crept into our decision-making.

As I write, I am thinking of Minka Hanskamp

and Margaret Morgan,* killed in South Thailand, and the Christians in Mainland China—to say nothing of the suffering new Christians in Cambodia. But my thoughts do not stop short at any point this side of the dissolution of the Times of the Gentiles, because as long as cruel dictators rule on earth, these and like situations will be with us. So let us look at what the Bible has to say about unrealized faith.

The book of Daniel introduces us to three men—Hananiah, Mishael, and Azariah. (By the way, I wish we could get these names into our heads instead of Shadrach, Meshach, and Abednego, which were the names given them to expunge the significance of God from their family designations.) It was the decree of Nebuchadnezzar, the dictator, that all men must bow to his image or burn in his fire that brought these three men into prominence. Because they would not comply with the command, they were brought into a dramatic confrontation with the powerful monarch. Though threatened with a horrible death, the three heroes refused to consider the fire as a factor in the case, turning rather to look to God and their spiritual resources. The stark, cold-blooded courage of Hananiah, Mishael, and Azariah as they face the frothing fury of Nebuchadnezzar has always been a puzzle to the world. But it should

*Their story is told in *Minka and Margaret*, by Phyllis Thompson: OMF Books, 1978.

not be to the Christian who grasps the reality of the springs of spiritual resource found in the Word of God. With their backs to the wall, Daniel's three friends calmly gave their testimony of faith in two strong positives and an alternate: "Our God is able to deliver us . . . and he will deliver us . . . *But if not* . . . we will not serve thy gods, nor worship the golden image which thou has set up" (Dan. 3:17, 18).

Faith's alternate, introduced by the words, "But if not," is no less an expression of faith than the two previous assertions. It gives, in fact, a demonstration of the reality of the faith they professed. In no way were they qualifying their statement or weakening the force of faith's first claims. Far from it. By adding to it an opportunity for God to take another course for achieving His glory at their expense, they were giving it a new dimension.

Just suppose for a minute that Hananiah, Mishael, and Azariah had stopped after claiming, "Our God will deliver us," and God had responded to their demand. They would have been saved, but the king's heart would not have been changed. There would have been no public acclamation of God as the great God of deliverances. God's superiority might not have been attested. And the three men would have missed the presence of the One like to the Son of man sharing the fire with them.

Furthermore, think what Minka Hanskamp and Margaret Morgan would have missed through the

long months of their torturous existence in the
hands of evil men, to say nothing of the thousands
of others in like circumstances. These would all
have missed the example of the power of faith's
alternate. In giving expression to their defiant
"But if not," the Hebrew exiles were insisting that
mere physical deliverance from the cruel crunch
of circumstances is less important than God's
rights to dispose of them according to His will.
This was their way of giving God an opportunity
to contradict their expectations if that was His will
and also of admitting that God was greater than
their interpretations of Him.

An escapist generation reads security, prosperity, and physical well-being as evidences of God's
blessing. Thus when He puts suffering and affliction into our hands, we misread His signals and
misinterpret His intentions. The prod to escape
from situations we are afraid of comes from Satan
through self. Peter urged the Lord Jesus to skip
the sufferings of the cross. To have yielded to the
temptation would have robbed God of His victory
weapon—the very weapon He had planned to be
used in crushing the serpent's head. Recognizing
the source of the temptation, Jesus turned to Peter
and said, "Get thee behind Me, Satan."

Faith's alternate is that deep primary motivation
that relates earth's afflictions to the Word and will
of God on one hand and to His sovereign right to
work for His glory in His own way on the other.
Confronted by Nebuchadnezzar's threat, Daniel

and his three friends faced God's clear command: "Thou shalt not bow down...." God doesn't supply cushions with His commands. If every command has to have a promise of deliverance to cushion the rugged absolute quality of its implications, God would be deprived of the powerful testimony of a faith that refuses to bend at the decree of any tyrant. Pastor Wang Ming-tao of Peking asked for no cushion when he was put under pressure to compromise. This was his testimony: "As I obey the Lord whom I have served and as I keep the truth which I have believed, I will not obey any man's command that goes against the will of God. I have prepared myself to pay any price and make any sacrifice, but I will not change the decision I have made."

A large proportion of our Christian enterprise has lacked this significant note. C. H. Nash puts it this way: "In face of the appalling happenings of the present day, we are being steadily compelled to realize that only through a fresh baptism of sufferings can the church be purged and fitted for the task which still confronts it in the evangelization of the non-Christian world.... The decisive battle of Christian truth ... is yet to be fought. The enemy confronting the church will be armed with every kind of destructive device which human ingenuity can invent and diabolical subtlety devise; against which assaults the church will have nothing to present but the bared and helpless breast of suffering, and then it will be seen that ultimate victory lies with the weakest and not with the strongest. There is a call then for recruits in the army of the Lord who are prepared to enter the school of discipline and to give their lives without reserve to the exemplification of these ideals which our Master Himself put to the fullest proof and by which He overcame the world."

What we see as God's recklessness is His way of putting into human hands an instrument of victory that He has carefully chosen and wondrously shaped for defeating the enemy and bringing glory to His name. Though it may seem to be the hard way, God's way is the winning way.

24

Lions'-Den Loyalty

At least one important application of the book of Daniel either has been missed completely or is just being played low key. Almost everybody knows about the interpretation of the visions that indicate the power sequence through "the times of the Gentiles." But how many know about the application of the book to the spiritual issues involved in living for Christ in today's world? We can count the ten toes of the image, but we skip the very real now-significance of Daniel in the lions' den.

The opposing teams take to the field in the first verses of the book, and the contest continues through the historic period known as "the times of the Gentiles." Daniel was there at the kick-off. We are in the last mad scramble, with the clock running out and only seconds left to play. It is important to remember that we share the same time period with Daniel, the period in which God has committed the political affairs of the world into the hands of Gentile heathen rulers. And for our understanding, God reveals in the vision of the image the power succession that is to dominate the political course of the times of the Gentiles. This image, however, deals only with one level of world history—the political—delineating the sequence in the political line-up and describing the climactic windup and replacement.

Another line of application runs through the book. This God pictures, not in a dream, but in the enacted parable—Daniel in the lions' den and Daniel's friends in the fiery furnace. Just as the dream spans the whole course of the times of the Gentiles, the application of real-life teaching parables, I belive, also stretches through the duration of the same period. The lesson could be written in three words: VICTIMIZED, BUT VINDICATED.

While in their outward form there is variety among the world empires who have a place in the image—between the empires of Nebuchadnezzar and Nero, for instance—one aim is common to all: the VICTIMIZATION of God's people. Nebuchadnezzar begins by ordering the eradication of the distinguishing marks of the captive Jews. This he sets about to do by forcing them into Babylon's mold. He won't even allow God's name to be in their names. And it's Nebuchadnezzar who sets the pattern for the political super-powers during the times of the Gentiles. The world powers want nothing in God's Daniels to remind them of God. From the outset under Nebuchadnezzar through to the bitter and bloodthirsty end this is what the contest is all about.

The image Nebuchadnezzar erected on the Plain of Dura is different only in form, not in essence, from the modern-day demand on eight hundred million Chinese to worship a man. Korean Christians and missionaries had the same decision forced on them in World War II that Hananiah, Mishael, and Azariah faced. Some of them went to prison, and some didn't.

Nebuchadnezzar and Ashpenaz may think they are calling the plays for Daniel and his friends. In reality God gave Judah into the hand of Nebuchadnezzar. The light that He placed in the midst of the nations had been scattered into the darkness. We dare not ignore this purpose in the captivity. The church today that develops an "interiority complex" will soon find, too, that God has ways of scattering the witness. The disciples wanted to get back to the comfy all-together, God-in-the-midst situation in Acts 1, but Jesus is emphatic that such hopes would not be realized and that their place was the ends of the earth among the wild beasts. Only God would commit His precious treasure into the hands of a few feeble men and then send them as victims into the lions' den or as sheep into the midst of wolves. This is because God's last word is VINDICATION and His purpose salvation.

God can be reckless with the physical safety of His children because spiritual issues are more important than security and prosperity. And the

spiritual issue about which God is concerned is
loyalty, even to the bound of death. Why did God
leave Watchman Nee imprisoned in China? We
would have liked to see him released and brought
to freedom and safety. Because the light is for the
dark places. Because loyalty has priority over safety, endurance over escape.

In selecting His witnesses, God looks for loyalty. Some of Daniel's friends didn't make it. Daniel,
Hananiah, Mishael, and Azariah were chosen out
of a group (1:6). The other ten or twenty do not
appear on God's lists. They sink into self-chosen
anonymity. They have allowed the world to
decide their life style and to set their standards of
right and wrong. They have willed to sacrifice
their distinctive marks because they can't bear to
be different from the world. The lions' den is not
for them. *The lions' den is only for those with
lions'-den loyalty.* We need to ask ourselves, Am I
living with the world or as its victim? Am I
unnamed on God's lists, or am I willing to be His
chosen representative in some dark place?

25

The Eternal Symbol

It is through the constricted window of Hong Kong that the world tries to assess what is happening on the other side of the Bamboo Curtain. Christians are piecing together what little they can see in order to pray for the faithful remnant in China. But as we look through this window on China, a stubborn knot sometimes may tie up our thinking. I have people ask me why God allows such a vast population to be cut off from any Gospel outreach. His program is world evangelism; yet here is a large portion of the world's total population fenced off effectively from any adequate contact and denied mutual encouragement in the Gospel among themselves.

Can we say that God is the responsible Authority for this state of affairs? Why does He allow this situation to persist? It must be that "now we see through a glass darkly." The window lets us see things that have their true values obscured. To look only through this window will give us an unbalanced viewpoint, and it is this that warps our judgment. So we may expect to find in Scripture something to correct this lack of balance, and

we are not disappointed. Over against the narrow
window that shows a troubled world, God opens
"a door in heaven."

"Behold a Door Opened" (Rev. 4:1)

Exiled to "the isle that is called Patmos," John,
the aged apostle, looked out through his window.
He could see the Iron Curtain of his day ruthlessly
at work in opposition to God's program. He saw
"companions in tribulation." His window was like
our window: to look out was to wonder. For his
abiding comfort and ours also there was "a door
opened in heaven." What God intended him to see
through this door was calculated to remove once
and for all any doubts or fears from his mind.

Let us now share with John some of the "open
door" revelation. Looking through this open door,
the spiritual focus immediately sharpens on "a
throne set in heaven."

"Behold, a Throne Set" (Rev. 4:2)

The focus of Chapter 4 is on the Throne. The
door opens and John sees the blaze of glory. He
takes in one by one the things that relate to this
summit of Majesty:

"One sat on the throne" (v. 2).
"There was a rainbow round about the throne" (v. 3)
"Out of the throne proceeded lightnings" (v. 5)
"Before the throne there was a sea of glass" (v. 6)
"Round about the throne were four beasts" (v. 6).

So far the prepositions all indicate proximity. The thoughts revolve around the *activity* of the throne: "Thou hast created all things," But as we move into Chapter 5, we are led into the *heart* of the Throne. No longer do the prepositions range from one position to another. As the drama unfolds, we are directed to the central point "in the midst of the throne." The activity of creation yields to the authority of redemption. The elder says to John:

"Behold, the Lion Hath Prevailed" (Rev. 5:5)

There are two thoughts here that wrap up one principle: the mastery of the Lion, and the mystery of the Lamb.

The mastery is the result, a consequence. This is what has emerged at the climax of a course, "The Lion of the tribe of Judah . . . in the midst of the throne."

The mystery is the responsible cause. This is the factor that determined what the result would be: "A Lamb as it had been slain." The death was fresh, the attitude of sacrifice unaltered, and this is what John saw.

"The Lion . . . hath prevailed"—this is the *fact*. "A Lamb, as it had been slain"—this is the *foundation* for the fact, and God had laid the foundation before history's first page had been written.

The thing that impresses me is that God is allowing us to see through His open door, the vindication of His procedures. He points us to the ultimate mastery of the Lion so that we may understand the mystery of His procedures as seen in the Lamb slain.

Only the slain Lamb can become the prevailing Lion. This is the principle that dwells deep in this passage. Whatever the sacrifice and suffering of the present, the principle demands that those who follow the Lamb in His pathway down to the bound of death will find that the victim reigns. The way to the Throne admits of no change from the utter helplessness of a slaughtered sacrifice, for the pattern of the Lamb slain persists throughout, from the beginning to the closing scenes. Human symbols change and become increasingly more terrible. Be they lion, or bear, or leopard, or combinations of all these, they avail not to cause God to vary His pattern and change His symbol. His symbol is still unchanged: the Lamb in the attitude of having been sacrificed; that is, weakness taken to its limit in unresistance and total collapse. But through the bitter struggles with world powers, represented by the most fearful symbols, the Lamb emerges standing, conquering, riding, and reigning.

This does not mean that tribulation and suffering are accidents and miscarriages of God's program—that is the window view. Annihilation, liquidation, collapse may be the pattern on earth for segments of the church. But God's opened door into the "things which must be hereafter" interprets the gloom in terms of glory: "Be thou faithful unto death, and I will give thee a crown of life."

26

Fuel-less Fire!

The story of Moses and the burning bush is mother's-knee story-telling material in most Christian homes. Popular interpretation puts the emphasis on the marvel of a bush unconsumed in the midst of enveloping fire. And why not, for isn't this a contradiction of fixed natural laws? A desert bush with its leaves and twigs, cobwebs and bird's nests is combustible, a natural fuel supply for the desert Bedouin. Yet this fire rejects the bush as its fuel resource and blazes on unfading and completely self-sustained. The miracle is not so much in the bush as in the fire; yet the bush somehow has attracted our attention and closed our minds to anything more. God was not primarily trying to show Moses the bush, but His glory that can ignore, yea reject, the fuel potential of the bush and yet burn on. God is introducing not the burning bush but the fuel-less fire.

Before attempting further interpretation of this unfed fire, we must examine the context. God's revelation to Moses is not given apart from the context of his experiences. The focus is on a disillusioned man. Moses was a man in whose heart a fire of zeal to accomplish God's great mission had burned fiercely forty years earlier. Now he is a man of lost vision, faded passion, and waning purpose. His inner fires have burnt to ashes. It had been his high hope to right the injustices being meted out to his people by the Egyptians. But, for all his impressive natural abilities and high degree of training, he had impressed neither friend nor foe. Confronted with exposure, he had fled to the wilderness, his mission unaccomplished. Certainly a self-sustained fire could never be applied as a symbol of the man himself.

Moses knew from his own experience that he would never again be able to trust his own emotions to supply motive power for spiritual work. It is at this point he is confronted by the God of the fire and hears Him declare: "I am . . . the God of Abraham, the God of Isaac, and the God of Jacob. I have seen the affliction of my people . . . and I have heard their groaning and am come down to deliver them." God is showing Moses that the fire of His covenant faithfulness, of His compassionate concern for His people's condition, and of His sovereign purpose was not the feeble, fickle flame that Moses may have imagined because of God's long delay in delivering His people. His fire had burned on, regarding not and needing not human passion to feed it.

In 1965 the Overseas Missionary Fellowship, a fellowship stemming out of the China Inland Mission, celebrated its centenary. What's so exciting about a centenary? Surely nothing unless it is to call attention to the fire of God continuing in a habitat of His choice. Ours is a common bush, chosen to demonstrate God's covenant faithfulness, His concern, and His sovereign purpose.

Consider the Glory of God's Faithfulness

"I am the God of Abraham, and the God of Isaac, and the God of Jacob." God says: "Look to My covenant with your fathers and see that the fire of My faithfulness to this covenant is still burning today."

Hudson Taylor built the structure of the China Inland Mission on God's faithfulness. He claimed: "There is a God. He has spoken in His Word. He means all He has said and will do all He has promised." One ground for this confidence was the text, "Have faith in God," which he interpreted rightly to read, "Hold God's faithfulness." He had confidence neither in his own faith in God, nor yet in the accumulated faith of a hundred or a thousand workers to sustain the work. A thousand people could have faith in some bridge and be proved wrong because the object of their faith was unable to fulfill their expectations. There had to be adequate assurances that God would accept responsibility for the involvements of literal obedience to His command. "Seek ye first the kingdom of God, and His righteousness," He has promised, "and all these things shall be added unto you." The decades of the CIM/OMF's witness surely demonstrate the continuing fire of God's faithfulness. "He abideth faithful: He cannot deny Himself."

Consider the Grace of God's Compassion

"I have seen the affliction of My people . . . and have heard their cry." That there are more heathen unreached with the Gospel today than ever is no indication that God's concern for the lost is on the wane. The zeal that burned in the hearts of the missionaries of one hundred years ago is a worthy record. Yet it could never be said that Hudson Taylor's love and concern for souls provoked God to greater love or added fuel to that great fire. The bush was unconsumed. It contributed none of its potential to increase or stimulate God's fire. And today the call is to see the glory of God's mighty love that blazes on, though unrequited and undeserved, ever seeking any old bush in which to demonstrate itself. Let this love possess us and, melting our cold unconcern, move us to bring our love to the altar of willing sacrifice.

Consider the Goal of God's Purpose

"Come now therefore, and I will send thee unto Pharaoh, that thou mayest bring forth my people . . . out of Egypt." Tides of war and revolution sweep the world. Yesterday's allies are today's enemies. National borders change overnight. There are hostile forces at large in every country: communism—subtile, sinister, and spreading—flamboyant nationalism, often menacing in its attitudes to Western peoples; and ancient religions in aggressive revival programs. These all present massive imponderables to those planning world evangelism. Add to these the attitude of homeland churches. We are being psychologically conditioned by the "missionary-go-home" line. We are being educated to consider ourselves eligible to predetermine the limits of our spiritual sacrifices. Does the sum of all these factors affect the issue? Let us be sure of one thing: God continues to incarnate His redemptive purposes in human lives. He still calls, "Whom shall I send, and who will go for us?"

Let world conditions fluctuate or worsen; the fire of God's purpose burns on.

27

A Working Relationship

In creation God acts sovereignly and alone. But in the unfolding of His redemptive purposes, He wills it otherwise. He chooses to unite with Himself human instruments and share with them the excitement of creativity. The incarnation was part of the working out of this plan. In sending His Son to become man, God revealed in a new way His purpose to limit Himself to working in and through a relationship with man. The vital, indispensable part of this working relationship is prayer. God communicated His will to the Son in the intensive exercise of prayer that occupied so many of our Lord's nights in desert places. Then on earth, working according to His Father's will, the Human Instrument acted in the performance of signs and wonders, counting on the power he had requested in prayer because His will was one with the Father's.

This brings us again to this basic divine principle in prayer—that God unites His people with Himself in whatever He wants to do, first leading them to pray and then giving the thing for which He burdened them to pray. God's will is to send

rain on Ahab's drought-stricken land. He will not
act alone. He unites Elijah with Him in His
purposes by communicating to him His intention;
then when Elijah prays, God acts. Elijah could
bring a drought on Israel in the first place, not just
because he prayed the rain out of the sky, but
because he could first say, "As the Lord God of
Israel liveth, before whom I stand." He was not
initiating some self-conceived idea, but was acting
with God for the performance of God's will, as he
read in Deuteronomy 11, for just such a situation
as prevailed in his days.

The same principle is taught by the Lord Jesus
in His Upper Room discourse under the symbol-
ism of the vine and the branches. Abiding in Him
is the condition He established for our asking and
His acting. What had been set up as the working
arrangement between Himself and His Father is
perpetuated in the New Covenant-based relationship between Himself and His Church. It was to
be standard operational procedure.

In a world whose keynote is utility, the significance of prayer is generally judged from the visible results it achieves. To limit the function of
prayer to its utilitarian aspect is to make of it an
emergency convenience, something to which we
are driven, but not something to which we are
consistently drawn. We allow our emotions to
guide our praying and then become discouraged
when our prayers do not seem to be accomplishing anything. If we would have power in prayer,

we will need to be on our guard lest our emotions run us up a dead-end street by twisting our religious ambitions inward instead of upward. The great need is to be taught to discern God's spiritual goals in the circumstances God allows to come into our lives and those of others.

While every act of true prayer is a beginning in the doing of God's will, we are reminded that it is possible, having begun right, to end up asking amiss. "Thy will be done" must remain the heart of all prayer. God's will is not done automatically and arbitrarily on earth. The Christian has a responsible part to play under the terms God has set—to pray, with God's will his only goal. Paul prayed three times for his thorn in the flesh to be removed. Jesus prayed three times that the cup might be removed—but even as He prayed, He rejected His own will and pled with strong crying and tears, "Thy will be done!" For Him, life's purpose was self-identification with the purpose of the One who sent Him. No natural, self-born impulse was allowed to override God's supreme will.

The quintessence of prayer is the intertwining of the will of man with the will of God—but only on the basis of man's surrender of self-will and self-reference. The necessity of man's prayer is in no way due to a reluctance in God that must be overcome—nor is it the function of prayer to change God's will. Prayer is an interdependent exercise in which neither party in the relationship is dispensable. God has so conditioned His redemptive activity that man's prayer is the force that moves His purposing into motion. He waits for our ministry of willing according to His will to free Him to work that will. And while we know that everything in prayer depends on God, He would have us realize that everything also depends on us.

28

A Problem and A Prayer

The PROBLEM was God's. The PRAYER was Hannah's.

The problem was encompassed in the words, "The word of the Lord was precious in those days: there was no open vision." God could find no one through whom He could communicate His will to His people. All that He had for them was denied utterance. All that could have come to the people of the revelation of His will and purpose was shut off, to their loss.

The prayer was the focus-point, the relevant factor for the successful disposal of the will of God, the relating of the available potential in man to the problem of God. Without thoughtful meditation we will not be able to see this, for a casual reading of the story jerks us into feeling sorry for Hannah and disturbed at God's apparent heartless dealings. Twice we read, "The Lord had shut up her womb." It does seem to be an unnecessary and cruel tormenting of an innocent soul. Why should she be compelled year by year to face having her shame batted spitefully around among the hissing gossip-mongers? Why should this condition of hers be made the most prominent thing in her life? Even with the passage of time she is not allowed to forget her failure, for yearly "her adversary provoked her sore, for to make her fret."

The hard thing for us to understand is the way the Bible emphasizes God as the responsible cause of all this trouble. Yet this is the point where we must stop until we begin to perceive the purpose of God in thus engineering things in Hannah's circumstances. What God did was to place on her heart a burden that corresponded to the very burden that is on His own heart. Thus God's problem is made Hannah's problem without her realizing it. The man-child that God needs in order that His word may come to all Israel is the man-child for which she is being so remorselessly driven to pour out her soul in prayer. Hannah's shut womb and its concomitant shame are God's means for hedging her into wits' end corner. There she will eventually lay hold on Him in desperation for the very man-child that He seeks and is waiting to give.

The more I think of this, the more the fire burns in my soul. Surely there is justifiable parallelism between this Bible story of Samuel's birth and the situation we are beginning to be concerned about with regard to the lack of male applicants to missionary societies. It is not hard to see the problem of God. The untold millions are never out of His mind and heart. He has a message for them, but is denied the media necessary for the communication of that message. And at the same time the people are shut off from His revelation. If Hannah's burden corresponded to the burden on God's heart, then surely it is true that the burden of shame that we are being compelled to face corresponds to the problem about which He is concerned. I am quite sure that in later years Hannah learned to look back to all the provocation and bitterness with deep appreciation, for was it not through this that she was led into a cooperation with God that brought not only the answer to her need, but also the answer to God's need?

The thing that concerns me is that we have lost our sense of shame. To make it more relevant and personal: Have I just been coasting along, thinking that because we have been able to send out hundreds of new workers in the last few years, there will be more following automatically? Which of the workers on the field now is there as a direct answer to a prayer of mine to the Lord of the harvest to thrust out laborers? When I know God has a message for the millions and that He has men to send with that message in answer to my prayer, and I neglect to pray, it could be classed as a careless omission. But when He has commanded me to pray for this express thing, for me to neglect doing it puts guilt upon my soul.

The shame that might brand us as being unable to produce the results our forefathers in the faith produced is more than the shame of the corporate

body of the mission or church, it is my shame. It
tells me that I have not the faith to believe God will
fulfill His own word to thrust out as I pray. The
problem is mine and the sooner I begin to reckon
it as mine and start being concerned about it, the
sooner God will have His problem solved. If God
is driving me into a corner, if I am becoming
conscious of my failure in this regard, then let me
take courage from the story of Hannah, for it is at
that point that I am nearest to release. There is
only one thing between me and the answer to my
burden and that is the very thing over which I am
going to get to grips with God immediately. "Pray
ye therefore . . . that He will send forth laborers."

This is the testimony of what God has been
speaking to me about over the past months, and I
truly believe that the answer is on the way,
already released from God's hand to the hand of
faith. Hannah's testimony is my testimony. "For
this child I prayed, and the Lord hath given me
MY PETITION which I asked of Him. . . ."

29

The Christian's Vital Breath

The poet of the 1970's would hardly describe prayer as "the Christian's vital breath," as James Montgomery does in his hymn on prayer. With some exceptions, prayer today is but a sickly caricature of the full-blooded reality that is seen in the Bible and in the biographies of men of God.

While Fraser of the Lisu may not have originated the idea of the missionary prayer letter, he certainly capitalized on it. His value-system put the little band of prayer helpers at the top of the list. They were God's effective means for achieving results through his work in the wild mountainous region of the upper Salween River. His own place was secondary to theirs even though he was the missionary in direct contact with the people. The priority task, as he came to see it, was to gather information and forward it regularly to the ones at home who were better able to give themselves to the business of winning the victories through prayer. Results vindicated his vision. Whole villages of Lisu people hitherto unresponsive and bound by Satan suddenly warmed to the Gospel. They sought his help in burning their fetishes and asked him to come to teach them the truth.

A reference to Paul only serves to confirm this pattern. "The vital breath" of the Philippian Christians brought a complete reversal in an impossible situation. Their supplication channeled "the supply of the Spirit of Jesus Christ" that saved things for Paul. Was he imprisoned in Rome, the goal-city of a lifetime's longing and strategy planning? Then it would be through the prayers of his friends in the churches that the apparent disaster to the cause of Christ would be turned about and made to bring blessing.

Could the prisoner trust the Philippian Christians for the right kind of praying, that quality of intercession that would bring the strong tides of salvation sweeping into the ranks of the Praetorian guard? Yes, he could. He was certain of that. "I know," he affirms, "that this shall turn to my salvation through your prayers."

The missionary had prepared his supporting friends for the exacting kind of ministry that would be expected of them. Read his letters—"We wrestle not against flesh and blood. . . ." "Praying always with all prayer and supplication in the Spirit, and watching thereunto with all perseverance. . . ." "Praying for us that God would open unto us a door of utterance. . . ." Strong, urgent, intense words; words that burst from him in holy originality, taking their color from the strain of contest and struggle-agonizing, laboring fervently, wrestling—these formed the backbone of his teaching on prayer for the churches.

The church today seems to be calling for disproportionate attention to the quality of the action in the place of direct contact, obscuring and belittling the priority work of prayer warfare. The imbalance is too patent to allow any glossing over. Look close to home and see what is happening in the churches you know.

Is the women's sewing circle a bigger thing than the prayer meeting? What about the men's breakfasts? How many of the regular attenders are as enthusiastic about prayer for the church's evangelistic outreach in the community? In the whole life of the church what sort of contrast is there between the time and interest shown in seminars, activities, and services and the time given to prayer? If an outsider were to attend our church prayer meeting, would he get the impression that we are a mutual comfort society, concerned only with each other's aches and pains? Or would he see us as a group vitally concerned for the salvation of lost men and women?

I cannot help wondering what has happened to "the vital breath." Isn't this what we are missing today? Haven't we discovered that the technical excellence we are developing is still relatively powerless to produce the right kind of results? I believe that stronger and quicker development in

God's work is impossible apart from multiplying prayer helpers filled with the spirit of Paul's strenuous prayer words.

What is it going to take to restore the balance and give the right kind of praying the right place of priority?

- It will take a discipline that will be contested by almost every aspect of today's life. The TV, the telephone, the banquets, the recreation, and even church activity will need to come up for review.

- It will call for a sacrifice of that quantity we call TIME that everyone is short of, yet sinful in wasting.

- It will take deep desire, so that the intensity of Paul's wrestlings may be duplicated in my longings after God's goal and in my prayers.

Given this spirit and pastors who are qualified to teach this kind of praying (alas! they seem to be getting fewer), we will begin to achieve our impossible goal and recapture

"the Christian's vital breath."

30

Discipline Accepted ...
Mission Accomplished!

Who is not aware today of the dropout of missionaries from their fields? A missionary returns to the field fresh from furlough, but within two months is on his way home again. A new worker only just out of language school and on his first station has to come home in less than a year from the time of his farewell meetings in his homeland. These could be members of any mission, denominational or interdenominational.

So we pose a problem: What kind of person can be expected to press through the accumulations of strain to finish his course? Is there some character quality that we must look for before we accept anyone for overseas service? Is there some kind of processing that will expose the potential one-term missionary so that he may be sieved out on the homeside before he has a chance to release a flood of troubles on hard-pressed fellow workers? Alas! the quality of spiritual temper that will endure the pressures of life in a foreign country is not easily discovered. The needed stress-resistance is not something that can be registered on some man-made grading system.

However, there was One who claimed, "I have finished the work Thou gavest Me to do." If our question is to be answered, it will not be through philosophizing. It will be found in a live experience of a man mixing with men in all the strains and antagonisms of fishbowl living. In the face of every kind of opposition, Jesus Christ was able at the end of His earthly ministry to report back, MISSION ACCOMPLISHED. More important than this claim, and complementary to it, was the comment of God Himself on the life of His Son. Scripture says, "He learned obedience," and so Heaven records, DISCIPLINE ACCEPTED.

Here is our answer. *His mission was accomplished because the discipline was accepted*, and the discipline was accepted because He wanted to finish His mission. Paul speaks of the dying of the Lord Jesus. This is not so much in reference to His death on the Cross, as to the daily dying that characterized His whole life. He consistently refused to live for Himself. Dying to the devil's lure of self-preservation, He refused to make bread for Himself out of stones. Dying to the temptation of an easy way to the crown, He resisted Satan's plea to throw Himself from the pinnacle of the temple. "This shall never be to Thee," was Peter's blunt response to Jesus' teaching on the necessity of His sufferings and death. "Get thee behind Me, Satan," was Jesus' stern reply. The treasure He guarded was more than His life; it was His dying. To have relinquished this dying at any point in favor of some escape scheme would have forfeited for Him the right to claim MISSION ACCOMPLISHED.

Surely this principle applies to anyone who would follow Christ. This, in fact, is just what He was getting at when He said, "If any man will come after Me, let him deny himself, and take up his cross daily and follow Me." The one who will go through to the end with steady pace is the one who accepts the daily discipline of dying, choosing to renounce and repudiate the competitive voice of self. This is what God seeks from those who serve Him.

Life is a two-sided affair. One side is idealistic, the other practical. The missionary's call to serve God is in the area of the idealistic. At first all seems vague and uncertain. But as the vision becomes clearer, it grows stronger, until it masters us. When things are this far along, we bring our call, as we conceive it, down to the level of the practical and place it alongside our natural abilities and personal preferences. Then we adjust our education so that it may bring some useful contribution to the great ideal and settle down to become a linguist, nurse, doctor, or educator. The goal ahead inspires us; the fire within drives us. We press forward with zeal and conviction, impatient and intolerant of anything that threatens to impede our progress. At this stage *mission* is the important thing. And because the job has a Cloud-Nine spiritual aura about it, we poke our heads through into thin air unconcerned about the merciless blunderings of our hot feet down on the earth.

In other words, we live in one dimension and tend to forget the practical matter of relating life's ideals to the business of ordinary living with all sorts of crazy people. It is to sharpen our attention to this practical side of the missionary call that God sends disciplines into our lives. It is here that things seem altogether awry. Why does God have to mediate His disciplines through the clumsy and unsympathetic hands of those we dislike and despise and whose authority we resent? We need discipline, granted—but why cannot it be delivered through acceptable channels?

We would like to ignore the discipline as unnecessary for us in particular, but nice for those who are not as far advanced spiritually as we are. Our missionary vision is clear: we are all ready for whatever lies ahead and are cocksure that we will not be one of those coming home to stay after the first term of service. So by our attitude we deny God the chance to say of us, "He learned obedience." God purposes to build into us the quality of endurance. In order to do this, He has selected the things we suffer at the hands of our fellowmen. The process of adjusting to the vagaries and limitations of those we are forced to live with does mellow and mature the character. The business of bearing about in our bodies the dying of the Lord Jesus is the way the idealist has his vision transmuted into the kind of living that counts in the murky world of human relationships.

The problem we posed at the beginning does have an answer. The one who will stay with his assignment through thick and thin is the one who carries this record: DISCIPLINE ACCEPTED. He is a man who is more concerned to guard his daily dying than his living rights. The hold a man's mission has upon him may be measured by balancing DISCIPLINES ACCEPTED against DISCIPLINES AVOIDED. Any man whose record seems to weigh heavier on the "Disciplines-Avoided" side should be considered a risk, not one to be encouraged to pursue applying for missionary service. Such a man is spiritually unrealistic. God's man is the man who accepts the daily dying because he recognizes this as an indispensable and integral part of seeing his mission accomplished. If we want to be used of God year after year in the place of His appointment, then let us welcome the incompatibilities that toughen spiritual temper and at the same time drive us to the resources of the Life that was laid down for us.

31

God's Scramble Squadron

In the pursuit of victory it sometimes falls to the lot of one particular branch of the armed services to bear the brunt of the enemy's attack and then to bleed and blast its way through to victory. The Battle of Britain in World War II is a good example of this. The collapse of France had cleared the way for Hitler to move ahead with Operation Sea Lion, his code name for the invasion of Britain. As the massive formations of his bombers and fighter escorts stormed into the skies over England, it soon became apparent that the survival of Britain was hanging by a very slender thread in the hands of the vastly outnumbered fighter pilots of the Royal Air Force.

As soon as the personnel in operations control spotted enemy planes on their radar screens, they would telephone the command, "Scramble!" to the RAF defense squadrons stationed along the line of enemy attack. When the order to scramble reached the pilots on the ground, it meant a desperate, mad scramble to win for themselves a position of advantage *above* the attacking planes. The race they must first win if they were to shoot the enemy out of the skies was altitude, and they gave this all they had as they clawed their way upwards.

There was no such thing as instant altitude for the fighter pilots of the RAF. Not so for God's scramble squadron. The believer has been granted the privilege of instant altitude by faith for any and every situation. If we are to grapple, not with flesh-and-blood adversaries, but with principalities and powers in the heavenlies, we need to come to grips with one basic truth of God's Word: that when God raised Jesus Christ from the dead and set Him in the seat of authority "far above all," He made us co-sharers with Him in every stage of the mighty finished work and then seated us with Him.

From only one position is it safe to approach and resist Satan, and that is from this position in Christ in the highest heavenlies. From this position Satan and his hosts are completely vulnerable.

So for us also altitude is a vital factor. Victory depends on it. Understandably, therefore, Satan's craft is dedicated to luring us away from this place of advantage and causing us to forget his vulnerability. The significance of being made powerful in the Lord is directly connected to the faith that maintains its position "far above all" in all circum-

stances and puts on with prayer Jesus Christ as the
only adequate armor of God.

These thoughts were triggered in my mind by
the things that were happening to me. During
1977 I had been having problems with my health,
but no one seemed to know what was actually
going on. Then in January, 1978, after I had gone
through another battery of tests, I was told that I
have amyotrophic lateral sclerosis, a rare disease
known among laymen as Lou Gehrig's disease.

I am sure the devil counted on this diagnosis as
something he could use to persuade me that my
active service in God's army was over and that I
should hunt up a clover paddock and enjoy what
was left of life.

History was repeating itself. Forty-two years
earlier he had been given a similar opportunity.
When I first applied to the China Inland Mission, I
was turned down. The reason given me was the
fact of my mother's death on the mission field, and
this was something I could do nothing about. It
was then that the devil tried to persuade me to
settle down at home and forget the whole missionary business. After all, I had done all I could do to
become a missionary and God had not helped—so
why should I persist?

But I refused to take the tempter's bait and to
accept my rejection as God's last word. I was sure
that He was just testing my sureness that He had
guided in my application to the CIM. And I was
right, for after a year the decision was reversed,

and I set sail for China as a member of the China Inland Mission. I learned from that experience to look to God as the First Cause in the things that happen to His children and to refuse to look at second causes.

So in 1978 [the author died in July 1978, shortly after this was written], instead of scouting around for a luscious clover patch in which to get fat and lazy, I have concentrated my thinking on the purpose of that mighty victory at Calvary and the implications of this for the Christian—for me.

As all Christians do, I live in a world where sin runs rampant. Yet God's Son was manifested to destroy the works of the devil. In the ascension God positioned His Son in the one seat of undisputed authority, far above all principalities and powers and every name put forward to challenge His authority. Because we share the seat with Him, He has delegated His authority to us as His representatives here on earth.

But some do not get excited at the privilege of instant altitude and instant authority with the all too obvious implications of conflict. Many Christians prefer the way of the world and would rather set up dialogue with the enemy on strategic arms limitations. That is fighting upwards. When we fight that way, the enemy has the advantage. We win only when we fight downwards.

With the roar of enemy attack filling the air— when our world seems to be crumbling around us—we must not lose our true character as those

united with Christ. Each of us needs to find out
what particular spiritual ministry God has
appointed us to perform in His name (even to be a
part of His "scramble squadron")—no matter
what our circumstances. He glories in His Body,
the Church, when it is "terrible as an army with
banners."